ENDORSEMENTS

"Loose to Live is the roadmap that will take desperate, frustrated, and hurting women from a place of despondency to walking in their divine purpose and becoming the best versions of themselves. This potent and life-transforming masterpiece is not simply a compilation of soul-searching poems but is carefully designed to influence the empowerment and transition of women from dormancy to progress. The poems, prayers of confession and scriptural application will serve to rip away the façade that disguises the struggles and impedes growth and propel us into a life of power and great successes. This book is a timely reminder to women, of the greatness that resides in us. We do not have to accept defeat and failure as a way of life and merely exist. It's time to arise and live; ***Loose to Live*** will show you how."

Nordia Stewart
Operations Manager
Gulfstream Petroleum SRL

"Heartiest Congratulations to Chevonette James-Henry on the writing of this powerful book, ***Loose to Live***. I believe that this was divinely orchestrated for such a time as this. Having experienced hurt both in my relationship and the church, I have discovered that there are many men and especially women who are hurting physically, emotionally, spiritually and psychologically in Christendom and are bound by the spirit of unforgiveness, resentment, low self-esteem and anger.

I believe that this book addresses real issues. When read, individuals will be equipped with the knowledge to break shackles and bondages, which brings deliverance. Rise and be healed as you immerse yourself in the pages of ***Loose to Live***.

I not only heartily commend the author of this book but I highly recommend it to everyone. It will be therapeutic and transformative for anyone who reads it."

Cossett Grey
Associate Pastor
Boulevard Church of the Nazarene

"This book is exceptional. It's no exaggeration to say it shines through on every page. What I liked were the confessions. Sincere and honest with an eloquent appeal. The book is an excellent investment. It will provide many hours of a new understanding and appreciation of life's challenging journey.

Powerful, uplifting, life-changing…a few of the words that come to mind when I opened the pages of ***Loose to Live*** and discovered the words of inspiration and hope that leaped from the pages. Our world is full of women who are simply surviving but not truly living, although created by God to do extraordinary exploits. ***Loose to Live*** was divinely written under the influence of the Holy Spirit to assist wives, mothers, sisters, daughters and all females to get past our past, unmask and rise above the ashes in our lives by the power of Almighty God. As these well-articulated poems soak into the very fibre of your being, no doubt some tears will flow, but you will experience healing, deliverance, liberation and victory as you finally break out and break forth into your purpose."

Desreen M. Smith
Director, Human Resource Audit –
Office of the Services Commission
Committee Member -
Women of Purpose Conference 2019.

"***Loose to Live*** has smashed the pretensions, poverty of spirit, private pain, and purposelessness that have paraded themselves and have chained many women of all ages, stages and statuses. Admittedly, James-Henry is a channel that God has used to expose and then heal, as she has touched an exhaustive list of issues familiar to women who have tried to endure but were only kept bound. Every woman should have a copy of this book because it is a key to a treasure chest found…when opened will help women to be loose to live."

Dr. Tesha M. Thompson, JP
Teacher Educator in the Dept. of Modern Languages at Shortwood Teachers College, Author of Broken for Service and other books, Founder of She's Royal Foundation, Founder and CEO of Trésors et Cadeaux and My Christian Events Consultancy and Products.

"This book and its insights are necessary at a time such as this when many women suffer silently in our pews. Many are sweetly saved but in need of deliverance and deep level healing from the burden of past errors or even psychological childhood inflictions.

I recommend **Loose to Live** as a must read if you are serious about the abundant life in Christ as a woman and the need to invite others to join us on this journey of growth and fulfilling our God-given purpose and passion."

Rev. Valerie V. Blake
Guidance Counsellor
Pastor, Elim Open Bible Church

"I identified with similar struggles brought up by the author of **Loose to Live**. Namely, finding life's purpose, self-doubt and being accepted. While other issues have a tangible beginning and hence a tangible solution, living every day doubting yourself, your abilities, your existence is like a slow malignance, eating away a bit of who you truly are with each passing day.

I perfected the art of the smile, the reassuring "I'm fine" when asked. But I couldn't escape the internal distress that I was living below my potential, that there is more, that I am more...... There is no clearer mirror than the actions of a child, and so as I began to see the same characteristics in my offspring, I knew, no matter how long the process I had to rise up and be.

This book reiterated that and gave tools/prayers for such. So today, I choose to be who I was created to be, loose and ready to live."

Kimberley Hamilton-Brown
BSN. RN

"This book is exceptional. It's no exaggeration to say it shines through on every page. What I liked were the confessions. Sincere and honest with an eloquent appeal. The book is an excellent investment. It will provide many hours of a new understanding and appreciation of life's challenging journey."

Debbie Ann Kerr-Scott
Attorney-at-law

CHEVONETTE JAMES-HENRY

ChevHen Press

Copyright ©2019 by Chevonette James-Henry
Loose to Live / Chevonette James-Henry

Printed by ChevHen Press
eMail: chevhen99@gmail.com

ISBN: 978-1-947671-77-5

All rights reserved. No part of this publication may be reproduced, distributed, or transmitted in any form or by any means, including photocopying, recording, or other electronic or mechanical methods, without the prior written permission of the publisher, except in the case of brief quotations embodied in critical reviews and certain other noncommercial uses permitted by copyright law. For permission requests, write to the publisher.

Scriptures unless otherwise stated taken from the HOLY BIBLE, NEW LIVING TRANSLATION, Copyright© 1996, 2004, 2007 by Tyndale House Foundation. Used by permission of Tyndale House Publishers, Inc., Carol Stream, Illinois 60188. All rights reserved. Used by permission

Cover and interior design by D. E. West, ZAQ Designs & Dust Jacket Creative Services
Cover photo by Derron Wright, D Wright Focus Photography

Printed in the United States of America

Dedication

I dedicate this book to my daughter, Joi-Ann D'Andra Henry. You have been my inspiration for many of the journeys I've embarked on. May you always know that 'No Infirmity is greater than God's grace.'

My sons Jon-Mark Anthony Henry and Jor-Dan D'Andre Henry, may you marry 'powerful, loosed' women and may you always facilitate growth in them as they continue to mature and evolve.

My sisters Naomi Walters-Grey and Angella Bowyer-Tubbs, two of the most powerful women I know.

My Mother-In-Law, Valdel Young and my Aunt Azeala 'Mell' Fearon who epitomize strength, power and grace.

TABLE OF CONTENTS

Foreword xvii
Preface xix
Acknowledgement xxi
Introduction xxiii

Section 1 – Jesus Wants to Loose You 1
Chapter 1 – Sin 3
   Secret Sins 4
   Secrets in the Room 6
   Lying 9
   Stealing 11
   Gossiping 13
   Anger 15
   Abortion 17
Chapter 2 – Hurts 21
   Father Wounds 21
   Tears 24
   Rejection 26
   Blindsided 29
Chapter 3 – Failure 33
   Falling Short 34
   Destined to Fail 36

Chapter 4 – Unmet Expectations 39
- Unplanned Life 40
- Prescription Life 42
- Unfulfilled Life 44
- Uncertainty 46
- Childless 50
- Death 52

Chapter 5 – Confusion 55
- Finding Jesus in the Gray 56
- Drowning 59
- Sleeplessness 61

Chapter 6 – Bondage 65
- Prisoner in my Home 66
- Stripped 67

Chapter 7 – Brokenness 71
- Broken 72
- Broken Dreams 75
- Crushed 77
- Damaged 79

Chapter 8 – Insecurities 81
- False Security 82
- Insecurities 84
- Sometimes 86

Chapter 9 – Aging 91
- Growing Old…Alone 92
- When the Girls Sag 95

Chapter 10 – Hiding 99
- Alcoholism 100

Wealth 103
Behind the Mask 105
Masked 108
Smiling Through It 111
Faking It While Making It 113

Chapter 11 – Loneliness 117
Emptiness 118
When He Cheats 119
Adultery 121
Married…But in the Dark 124
Broken Picket Fence 127

Chapter 12 – Unhealthy Emotions 131
Depression 132
Indecision 134
Sadness 136

Chapter 13 – Victimization 139
Abused 140
Raped 142
Black Sheep 144
Utterances of Destruction 146

Chapter 14 – Struggles 151
Jobless 152
Toiling 155
Penniless 157
Weight-Gain 159
Weight-Loss 162
Illness 164

Section 2 – Loosed **167**
    Loose 168
Chapter 15 – No Greater Love **171**
    Wrong Address 172
    He Wants Me 175
    He Chose Me Long Before 178
    Chosen 180
    Masterpiece 182
    Inscribed in His Hands 184
    Apple of His Eyes 187
    Favoured 189
Chapter 16 – Wanting Something New **191**
    Who I'm Created To Be 192
    Wanting Something New 194
    Searching 197
    Whispers of the Lord 199
    Getting Passed the Past 201
    Let it Go 203
    Naked Before the Lord 205
Chapter 17 – Becoming Me **209**
    Becoming...Me 210
    From Rags To Riches 212
    Connecting With Jesus 214
    He Takes My Mess 216
    Woman...You are Loosed 218
    Loosed to Live...Nothing Else Matters 220
    Loosed to Praise 222
    Loosed to Succeed 224
    Loose to Walk in Authority 225

Chapter 18 – Freedom **229**
    Freed 230
    Freed from Prison 232

Chapter 19 – New Beginnings **235**
    The Inner Court 236
    A New Day 238
    ...Only God 240
    Beyond Our Limitations 243
    Dreaming Again 246
    Makeover 248
    My Spiritual Closet 252

Chapter 20 – The Change **257**
    No Longer A Slave…. 258
    Despair to Deliverance 260
    Resting In Him 262
    Quiet Rest 264
    Peace in Christ 266
    Phenomenal Woman 268
    Divine Legacy 270
    Moving Beyond the Trajectory 272

Chapter 21 – Tributes **275**
    Becoming the Signature Woman 276
    Powerful Women 279
    Signature Woman...Connections 281
    My Story...Your Story 283
    Phenomenal You My Sister Who Mothered Me 285

About the Author 289

Foreword

When Chevonette James-Henry, a Signature Woman, asked me to review and endorse her book *Loosed To Live,* I knew it was something extraordinary in the making. This was in God's divine plan.

To learn that the penning of this book resulted from her personal encounter with God at the *Signature Woman Leadership Connection - 2017,* the theme of which was *Loosed To Live,* comes as no surprise. While the event was impactful, liberating and transformational, I knew that the process of taking God's daughters from fear and self-preservation, to healing, restoration and transformation - to living fully alive – was only beginning. Chevonette's book, *Loosed To Live,* is a timely and significant part of this continuing process.

Many of us are bound emotionally, relationally and spiritually. We protect ourselves behind masks that have become comfortable and reliable, so much so, that we are often unaware of the deleterious impact this has on our ability to live fulfilled lives. We therefore fail to take the steps towards healing and restoration.

This powerful and transformational book is a wellspring of vital truths and insights designed to bring healing to our deepest wounds, liberation from our darkest fears and forgiveness for our secret sins. As we prayerfully and purposefully peruse each page we will find the courage to lower our masks. We will discover that under our masks lie extraordinary persons created in the image of an extraordinary God designed to live extraordinary lives.

What Chevonette has managed to do in the pages of this book is fascinating. Poetic contemplations, confessions and profound truths from the Word of God grace each page with honesty, precision and clarity. When you have finished reading this book "You will know the truth and the truth will set you free" in the most basic areas of your life, your goals, your motives and your understanding of your significance and true potential in God.

Read it. Learn from it. And, by the power of God's Holy Spirit, be Loose to Live it.

Claudette D Cooke Ed.D, CMT, CPC,CCRC
Corporate Vice President
Jamaica Broilers Group,
Signature Woman Leadership Connections,
Convenor

Preface

Nestled in St. Luke 13 (10-13) is an interesting story of an obscure woman. Very little is known of her, except:

- she had an infirmity
- her infirmity kept her (deformed, disabled) bent out of shape for over eighteen years.
- Her infirmity was placed on her by the devil.

I was struck by the enormity of the story and though I had read it many times before it lingered in my thoughts for weeks. It was during my 'umpteenth' reading that one truth suddenly jumped out at me, **her infirmity was not one she was born with**! Rather, it was one that was placed on her, not by a medical error or an accident, but by the devil himself. So, for eighteen years she was not only ' bowed' down but she was also 'bound', as if tied with a chain or very strong ropes which kept her from standing upright for those long, painful, frustrating and grueling years. This infirmity must have affected her spiritually, emotionally, financially and physically.

What an absolutely scary place for this woman to be!

I found it ironic that this woman may have gone to the synagogue (church) for possibly many months or years and yet, was still bound, that is, until she was loosed by Jesus. I'm imagining that she sat in the synagogue week after week, feeling sad, tired, weak, worn, dejected, rejected.

Sounds familiar???

Through my research (formal and informal), experience and observation, I have found that there are many of us (women) in the church who are bound by an infirmity (ghost from the past, broken relationships, poverty, life altering circumstances, etc.). Like this woman our infirmity has kept us from becoming who God wants us to be, kept us from achieving the destiny He has ordained from the beginning of time and kept us from walking upright and confident in the purpose we are called to pursue. Many of us are bound and struggling to believe that we can ever be loosed.

Having met Jesus in a very 'upfront' and personal way this woman found out that 'No Infirmity is Greater Than God's Grace.' That God cares for the wounded. God had the power to make her well and He had the power to loose her and set her free.

The good news is, like this infirmed woman, God wants to set us free!!!! Hallelujah!

Journey with me…
Be Challenged.
Be Inspired.
Be Empowered.
Jesus is ready…are You?

Acknowledgement

My soul-mate, partner, ride or die, best friend Andrew Anthony Henry, thank for encouraging me to be a woman of purpose, supporting me in my bid to discover the 'me' I was designed to be, for pushing me to chase my dreams…You are truly the wind beneath my wings.

Special Thanks to Jonelle Murray who edited the book and provided invaluable insights, critiques and perspectives.

My friends whom I have prayerfully selected to form my inner circle, your counsel, prayer and support have been invaluable.

My triune God, who has been my instructor and guide. I have grown and blossomed under your empowering tuteledge….my life makes so much sense because You are the center of it.

Introduction

There is a spiritual war raging around us, every second, every minute, every hour, every day. Satan is constantly attacking us, hurling lies and trying desperately to derail or stop us from achieving the plans God has for us. He does not want us to be who God created us to be, who we were destined to become. He knows if he can keep us thinking and believing we are incapable, invaluable, inadequate, unattractive, unwanted…he gains the upper hand…. he wins.

True, sometimes the struggles that we fight daily are so heavy and so deeply entrenched in our lives they become unbearable, life-altering and almost impossible to overcome. However, with Jesus at the center of our lives, prayer and declaration of the truth of God's Word we can make that important turn-around and walk in the destiny we were created for.

For years, I battled with extreme fears, feelings of never 'measuring up' and at one point I had very little self-worth. I combatted claustrophobia, "daddy issues" and self-doubt. I have spent over twenty (20) years rediscovering who I am, what I stand for and my life's purpose. I have found the freedom that comes with this discovery and have continued to focus on developing myself in all areas and living my dream of writing.

The benefits of this self-discovery have been astronomical. Not only am I living my dream, but I have proven that despite your origins or your struggles, anything, absolutely anything is possible. More importantly though I have discovered along the way that my life makes more sense when God is the center of it.

Loose to Live looks at some of the issues and challenges we go through as women and how they sometimes impair our potential and growth.

We will journey together through things in life that may break us and discover what God does in our brokenness to help us, strengthen us and bring beauty out of our broken situations.

Loose To live will heighten our awareness of many of the spiritual battles we face as women and show ways how to fight them with prayer, confession and declaration of the truth of God's word.

It's a great empowerment tool for individuals, small groups and church bible study. It may also be used to initiate discussions on topics that may seem taboo in the church but critical to our 'struggling' and even our seemingly 'got-it-together' women.

Written in simple everyday language, it is a must-read. Do not delay, get your copy, you will not be disappointed.

On November 18, 2017 I was invited to attend the Signature Women Conference in Kingston, Jamaica. Dejected, sad, worn I really did not want to be there. However, it was whilst there that I had the following encounter with God, with specific instruction to write this book.

DIVINE REVELATION

I sat in a conference today
when a divine revelation came my way
I came face to face with God
my Maker, my Lord
I saw things for what they were
and life was quickly brought into focus.

He showed me women
all dressed in white
surrounded by a really bright
light,

standing before God's throne
offering up praises to Him alone,
audible praise, hands held high
opened hearts allowing their spirits to fly.
jubilant faces
expressive adoration,
emotions clearly stirred
It was undiluted worship in action and word.

But as I looked closely I saw
that there were other women in the throng
they wore no jubilation, no happy expressions,
they seemed to be totally out of place
stress marring each tired, downcast face,
etched with sad defeated looks
as if life was on tethered hooks.
Though they were in the midst of the happy songs
they seemed to be the depressed ones
stressed, frustrated, and confused
and while others were praising
they seemed like spiritual
recluse.

I turn to the Lord with a questioning look
what is the meaning of this?
as my body shook,
then with bowed head
He said

'There are many women who
carry their burden like a crown
refusing to ever lay them down,
they are pressed down by many things
so nothing in their hearts ever sings,
they don't realize, I came and conquered
it all
and all they need is on me to call,
but yet they live defeated, lonely lives
filled with misery and strife.
And though the battles they fight daily are very real
they only need understand their fate is already sealed,
for I will take their burdens, if they will give them to me
that's the reason I died on Calvary.

As my Saviour spoke
before Him I broke,
because I too am guilty
of filling my life with worry,
of not trusting in His power
believing He is my mighty tower

So I asked God to forgive me
and set my spirit free
to offer Him total praise
for the rest of my earthly days.

A CHILLING TESTIMONY

In writing this book I decided to test the validity of the claims made that there are many Christians who, though saved, still struggle with "infirmities", that has kept them bound, some for many years. Nothing prepared me for what unfolded in one of my many meetings.

Lila (not her real name) was excited about our meeting, after all, one of her favourite girl was writing a book and she would be included.

As I shared with her what the book was about, I could sense a literal change in the atmosphere. The face which was a beautiful portrait of grace now seemed mangled and marred with obvious pain. For a while I was tempted to touch and shake her as she seemed locked in a moment of time. After what seemed like minutes but might have been seconds, she started to speak. Her voice was low, contorted and filled with raw emotions so thick you could cut it with a knife. I was baffled.

She shared about being molested by a family member when she was a teenager, how dirty and soiled she felt and still feel. She spoke (sometimes in an almost inaudible voice and I struggled to hear) about the nightmares which follow, about how it had damaged her self-esteem, her relationships and, for a time, her career….that was until she met Jesus. What was shocking though was that she had never told a living soul about the 'hell' she had endured.

Nothing, absolutely nothing prepared me for the sobs that followed. Heart wrenching, gut piercing sobs. And without meaning to, I too began to cry. So, there we sat, holding each other, rocking to and fro and crying.

I cried for this 87 year-old woman who had tried to live life but had never gotten over a wrong done to her over 70 years ago.

At the end of what was an emotionally taxing hour she said 'I feel free.'

This was just one of the many such stories I would be privy to….

SILENT CRY

I walk with head held high
but deep inside I cry
unseen pain
hidden wounds
silent tears
dark fears
unspoken horrors
nightly terrors
camouflaged well
yet creating a shell
of a woman.

I was a wounded girl
now a wounded woman
perpetuating the cycle

of mistrust
brokenness
unforgiveness
untapped potential
sadness
unfulfilled life.

I don't want to be like this
I desperately want to be loosed
to break out
to break through
to break forth
into that purpose
that seems elusive
to my naked eyes.

I am like a caged bird
yearning to be set free
to soar
unhindered by the
bars of a cage,
stuck in a place
it was never created to be
living by the hope that
one day
a Saviour will come to set it free.

SECTION 1

Jesus Wants to Loose You...

Are you struggling with sin, bad habits, doubts, depression, confusion?

Are you feeling used, abused, damaged, let down, abandoned?

Are you ready to give up, call it quits?

Journey with me as we:

- add imagery to those struggles that may exist in our lives.

- read poem/poems that bring the struggles to life.

- pray powerful prayers of confession.

- use the Word of God to quench the fiery darts of the enemy.

- be reminded that 'No Infirmity is Greater Than God's Grace'.

But He said to me, "My grace is sufficient for you, for my power is made perfect in weakness…2 Cor. 12:9 (NIV)

Chapter 1

Sin

Do you struggle with sin?
Do you find yourself with a divided heart?
Do you find yourself falling for the enemy's tricks over and over and over again?
Do you know that what you're doing is wrong, but find it difficult to stop?
Are you so tired of fighting, you have just given up?
Is the enemy telling you there is no hope?
Is it your desire to please God but your flesh seems to be winning?

Romans 7:23-24
But I see another law in my members,
warring against the law of my mind, and bringing me into
captivity to the law of sin which is in my members.
O wretched man that I am!
who shall deliver me from the body of this death?

SECRET SINS

Many sins are covered
underneath the hats we wear,
the titles we bear
the places we sit
the notes we hit,
the way we preach
the way we teach,
our eloquence
our persistence,
our willingness
our effectiveness,
the amount we give
where we live,
the shouts we make
the vows we take.
who we know
where we go.

Many secret sins are ignored
pushed out the door
or held in private
with no remorse,

but seem to
die a silent death
behind sealed lips.

Some are covered up
placed in a tightened cup
pretending it's not there
yet knowing its everywhere.
It's just easier
to wish them away
willing them to stay
away from the church.

CONFESSION

Heavenly Father, I confess all the secret sins in my life and ask that you forgive me for each one. I confess the sin of _____. Help me to renounce and turn away from this sin by your power. Thank You for not leaving me in darkness and shame, for showering me with grace, for showing me the way out. In Jesus' Name, Amen.

THE WORD

Psalm 90:8

*You spread out our sins before you - our secret sins—
and you see them all.*

SECRETS IN THE ROOM

All the girls were present that night
It was a meeting of powerful thoughts and minds.
a converging of women all dressed in white
wearing diamonds, pearls silken and bright.

On the outside we were a happy throng
we had it all together nothing seemed wrong.
we were projecting what the others needed to see
that life was great, full of laughter and glee.
but nothing was further from the truth
we were all hurting women
some of us since we were youths.

Sister Rape was present and trying not to cry
though she felt tormented and dirty on the inside
She was still hurting; the pain never goes away
a permanent tattoo on her heart pulsating and there to stay.

Sister Child Abuse had shown up
Oh, how hurt had filled her cup
she hated what she had become
in turn abusing her love ones
creating a never-ending cycle
of hurt and pain.

Sister Battered Wife still had her shades on

not only was it stylish
but it hid every single one
of the punches she had received
from her husband's hand.
Sister Unfulfilled was there
no one needed to know
that she was cheating on her husband
with the one next door.

Sister Mistress was quiet
she dared not open her mouth to speak
she wanted no one to know
that she was sexually weak
she was a side chick
a sexual freak.

Sister Prostitute sat wondering
how long before its night
she had a client waiting
for the shadows of the light.

Sister Alcoholic sat desperately craving a drink
keeping her lips sealed
knowing her breath stinks
of the drink she had just before coming in.

Sister Prescription Drug was already
dozing off
tired of pretending she had a permanent cough

which would explain away
the pills she downs every single day.

We all wore our secret well
hoping to no one Jesus would tell,
He alone knows the truth
that we were all imperfect beings
tasting forbidden fruits,
we each have good intentions
to be made perfect by Him
who could forgive our tons of sin
but….

CONFESSION

Lord Jesus, I'm tired of the sin struggle in my life. I renounce the sin of _____. You promised that if we will confess our sin, You are faithful and just to forgive us and make us clean again. Uproot and dig up the root of _____in my life. Cause that it will never spring to life again, in the name of Jesus. Lord, root out the darkness and light up my life with Your Holy Presence. In Jesus name I pray, Amen.

THE WORD

Psalm 19:12-13

*How can I know all the sins lurking in my heart?
Cleanse me from these hidden faults. Keep your servant
from deliberate sins! Don't let them control me. Then I will
be free of guilt and innocent of great sin.*

LYING

Lying spirits are everywhere
at the altar
in the aisle
in the chair
and mine is one of them.

I lie with ease
I lie to tease
I lie to deceive
I lie when I perceive
the truth is too much to handle.

No one is immune
I lie to friends
co-workers
well wishers
strangers.

Sometimes it's a little "white lie,"
made to try to make someone feel better
happier
steadier
worthy.

My lies are often deliberate
deceitful
deceptive

devious
unmerciful
mendacious.

I lie about personal achievements
accomplishments
success
whatever
whenever
however it fits a situation.

I need to stop
I really try
I cry and cry and cry
But the tears dry
And then the cycle
starts again....

CONFESSION

Heavenly father I confess that I am a liar. Forgive me for all the lies I have ever told. Forgive me for hiding my sins from you and covering up with excuses. Forgive me also for the lies I tell myself thereby opening the doors for the devil to attack my mind and body. Teach me to speak the truth always and to give honest answers at all times. In Jesus name, Amen.

THE WORD

Proverbs 12:22
*The Lord detests lying lips, but he delights
in those who tell the truth.*

STEALING

When I look in the mirror
I do not like what I see
I do not see an overcomer
staring back at me.
The Lord has spoken to me
many, many times
about my daily struggles
about this sin of mine.
I try hard to listen
and to do what's right,
but I'm never, ever victorious
so I willfully gave up the fight.

My heart is so badly broken
this sin is way too much to bear
now I'm daily losing my struggle
with this load I'm unable to share,
no one will understand
and I'm shaking with fright
cause no one can help me make this sin right.

How do I tell anyone
about this awful sin of mine?
How can I make them understand
that I've been struggling for
a long, long time?

How can I share this secret
so despicable
so vile
that I am a thief
without the willpower
to stop?
How do I tell them
I'm nothing like Christ? I see no work in progress,
no sign of God in my life?

How can I let them know
that each time I am weeping
I am desperately seeking
strength
to stop these hands from stealing.

CONFESSION

Lord Jesus, I am a thief. Help my hands to steal no more. Help me to use these hands to do only what pleases you in Jesus name. Bless the work of my hands that I may honestly work. I renounce stealing and all ties to stealing, in Jesus' name, Amen.

THE WORD

Ephesians 4:28
If you are a thief, quit stealing....

GOSSIPING

The church is full
of me, I have no mercy, I have no fear,
I talk about everything
I talk everywhere,
I know no justice
no one is spared
my tongue keeps me happy
my words spread fear
in the heart of anyone
whoever tries to cross me so,
though they know it's wrong
they all let me be.

I ruin families, marriages, careers
with rumours without cheer
I dismantle lives, relationships
through any available ears.
I tear down schools
churches, politicians
preachers, teachers
lawyers, accountants.

I am cunning, fearsome
I hit the ground running
malicious, deceptive

connective, receptive
I become deadlier as I age
I am unstoppable
amazed
by how gullible we all are.

I'm respected
connected
quoted
believed
admired by many
who share their deepest secrets,
runnings
happenings
longings
hoping that their secrets are safe with me.

CONFESSION

Lord, I admit that I'm guilty of talking behind people's backs. I know that I'm wrong for doing it. I ask Your forgiveness. Help me to keep a tight rein on my tongue and to refrain from gossiping about other people. I repent from my activity in gossip, and I turn from it in Jesus' name!

THE WORD

Proverbs 20:19

A gossip goes around telling secrets,
so don't hang around with chatterers.

ANGER

There is no calmness in me
when I become angry,
there's no safe place to be
when this feeling envelopes me.

It's way too big now
Don't know how
it ballooned to this degree
inside of me
encroaching on every
emotion
action
reaction
decision
my ability
to stay in touch with reality
to be
rational
logical
stable
able
to see
the 'me' I can be.

Now it's gone
way too far

I'm drunk with poison
and the horizon
seems bleak
steeped
with hatred
leaving me naked
to the onslaught
of my own mind.

This must stop
this vicious cycle of hatred.

I can't be a victim forever
this bond I must sever
This feeling must not remain
pulsating through my veins
polluting every thought
slaying every dream
chunking away
everyday
pieces of my heart.

CONFESSION

Loving Father, I place my struggle with anger and bitterness in Your hands. set me free from them, I pray. I confess that my anger controls my every thought and action but You are faithful and just to forgive the outbursts of anger in my heart and the actions that follow, and to cleanse me of all unrighteousness. Set me free from all that contribute to this anger raging in me. Thank You, in Jesus name, Amen.

The Word
Ephesians 4:31-32

Get rid of all bitterness, rage, anger, harsh words, and slander, as well as all types of evil behavior. Instead, be kind to each other, tenderhearted, forgiving one another, just as God through Christ has forgiven you.

ABORTION

I never meant for it to happen
but the protection was forgotten,
I was really careful,
hopeful,
but in the heat of the moment
I got caught up in the current
of emotions
flooding my heart and soul.
Now all I feel
is a shame that's real
sorrow
about tomorrow
guilt and fear

permeating the very atmosphere
refusing to leave
to my heart cleave
holding me hostage
day after day.

I took the pregnancy test
and I knew
that this unplanned child
of mine
could never be
left to survive.

I'm distraught
the man is long gone
he didn't stay around for long
as soon as he heard the news
he became an emotional recluse
gone back to his wife
his happy, sad life.

The world will shun me for sure.
If I share the truth,
They'll love me no more
"I can't have this child,
My life is a mess
I must do for him what I think is best.

now the years have

taken its toll
ruling my body and soul
bound in a cycle of unforgiveness
failing everyday the ultimate test
of believing I will ever recover
from my emotional hangover
for my heart is a daily lead
dead, dead, dead.

CONFESSION

God, I come to you broken and ashamed. I am sick with regret, sorrow and pain. Have mercy on me. I now come in the name of Jesus and ask complete forgiveness for the abortion(s) which I have had. I ask that with the precious blood of Jesus you would completely wash me. Cover me, my mind, my body, my past, my present and my future. Help me to forgive myself. Release me from the trauma and torture that takes place in my heart every day. May I feel Your forgiveness and love filling me and surrounding me, In Jesus' name, Amen.

THE WORD

Psalm 127:3-5

Children are a gift from the Lord; they are a reward from him. Children born to a young man are like arrows in a warrior's hands. How joyful is the man whose quiver is full of them! He will not be put to shame when he confronts his accusers at the city gates.

Chapter 2

Hurts

Every person who walks planet earth has been wounded. Some more than others. For many of us the pain we have suffered in our past is still impacting our lives now; and we can't fully embrace the new life God offers us because we're still stuck in a frustrating cycle of brokenness, hurt, anger and pain that leaves us feeling hopeless.

Psalm 34:18 The Lord is close to the brokenhearted; he rescues those whose spirits are crushed.

FATHER WOUNDS

Never met him
don't know what he looks like
still I see his face
I dream about him each night.
I'm bleeding, my wounds are open wide

though this man who produced me
is clearly out of sight.

I've yearned for him
though he left eons ago
still I wish I could feel his arms
around me thrown.

These feelings toward him
may seem to be dumb.
Cause though I'm sad, upset, confused,
angry, hurt, bemused
mostly I'm just numb.

Every girl needs her dad
but mine was never there
to talk about boys
or compliment me on my hair
or the clothes I wear.

I'll never understand why he felt he had to go
why he just disappeared though
he knew we loved him so.
He left so abruptly
never once looking back
taking all our hopes and dreams
not caring what we lacked.

Not caring that we'd be
tormented, trapped, and torn,
sorry for the very day we were born.

This anger engulfing me
Is like a bush fire raging wild
the hatred I have for him
dominates my heart and mind.
making relationships destructive and hard
I see it now
I'm severely scarred.

Now I realize
what he did to me.
crippled my ability
to be
anything but emotionally unhealthy

He ruined me,
made me cry,
he really hurt me,
made me want to die.

There is a deep hole in my heart
that no one sees
it continues to get deeper
since the day he left me.

So Daddy dear
I hope you can hear
your name been called
as you prepare for your fall
which is certain to come.

CONFESSION

Dear Lord, I want to forgive my father for abandoning me. I confess that I am still deeply hurt by his abandonment. I release all the pain and anger that I have been feeling for years, since childhood. God please take control of my life and help me to see and experience you as my 'Abba Father' who provides, protects, secures, comforts, supports and who loves me unconditionally. In Jesus name, Amen.

THE WORD

Psalm 27:10
*Even if my father and mother abandon me,
the LORD will hold me close.*

TEARS

My life is in shambles
I don't know where to begin
I have made so many mistakes
in my life of sin.
I've lied
I've cheated

LOOSE TO LIVE

I've made this life a mess
I fight so many demons
I'm disillusioned and depressed.

This life is full of struggles
lots of twist and turns
and while outside looks normal
inside is laced with burns.

I keep making really bad choices
especially about men
not caring that they ill-treat me
every single one of them.
It seems I wear a label
which screams, 'I'm weak and need a man
you need not treat me like a lady
I will always understand.'

So they heap all their crap
and place them in my lap
knowing I'm too weak to retaliate
though my heart is filled with hate.
You have no purpose in my life
except to bring mischief and strife
but I can't say goodbye
I don't even know why
so I cry and cry and cry.

CONFESSION

Heavenly Father I am struggling with my emotions right now and need your help. I give to You every feeling, unhealthy habit, choice, behavior that causes me to allow myself to be used and abused.

I refuse to believe every lie that tells me I do not deserve better that what I have been receiving. Restore my self-belief, my self-image, my self-esteem. In Jesus name, amen.

THE WORD

Psalm 27:5
For he will conceal me there when troubles come;
he will hide me in his sanctuary.
He will place me out of reach on a high rock.

·

REJECTION

You walked into my life
on a warm summer day
from the moment our eyes met
I knew you were here to stay.
You took me on a whirlwind romance
and no one could tell
it wasn't finally my
chance
at that thing called happiness.

You courted me
praised me
loved me
adored me
made me your queen.

We were inseparable, joined at the hips it seemed.
We went everywhere, nowhere was too far
whether we had to walk, take the bus or rent a car
You bought me anything and everything my heart desired
nothing was too expensive despite the price it required.

I loved you with every fibre of my being
and I was certain you loved everything about me.
you could do no wrong
you became my song
my salvation.
You reached a place in my heart
that was uninhabited by any man
It was held sacred reserved for that special one…you

Then it happened in an instant
starting with a very ugly rant
and went on and on and on.
Suddenly you had changed
became enraged
in a moment
in the twinkling of an eye
I couldn't understand it

what went awry?
What could make you say those awful things you did?
stupid, insipid
weak, spineless
useless, clueless
ugly, pudgy
fat, frumpy

Now you say, you're in love with me no more
I make you sick, I have no allure
it's bittersweet, what's happening to me
it came as a shock, hard for me to believe.
except
You let go of your pretention
and took away all my illusions
but Oh how it hurts...the pain of your rejection.

CONFESSION

Father God, I don't understand this situation. But I do understand Your goodness to me. I understand that You love me and Your love for me knows no limit, no boundary. Help me replace the fears threatening to consume me with truth. I am feeling so hurt, broken, torn, fearful, rejected and scared. Please help me with all these emotions. I give them to You and ask that You replace each one with Your joy, power and peace. In Jesus' name, Amen.

THE WORD

Philippians 15:13
I pray that God, the source of hope, will fill you completely with joy and peace because you trust in him. Then you will overflow with confident hope through the power of the Holy Spirit.

BLINDSIDED

This pain I'm feeling
has me reeling
twisted in a tight knot
tightly wrapped
unable to react
to the pain of you leaving
me alone
in our home
which was once our serene place of rest
laughter, delightful sounds of happiness.

Now the house is empty
and silence permeates each room
there is no sound of your voice
that loud boom.
I will hear your laughter no more
as you tickle me against the kitchen door
taunting me with those silly kisses
that would make me weak
without ever missing a beat.

I must forget the happiness we once shared
the thousand ways you showed me you cared
the little things you would randomly do for me
making me gleeful with your spontaneity,
how with one smile you could make me weak
sharing your thought without a single speech
proving our compatibility
was your daily realityas we built life from nothing
while knowing we had everything
we needed to be
that success story
The Ones who made it.

I never saw it coming
But,
It's all over
time to move on
now you're making a new life with a new woman
I must rise from the ashes
without hesitation
Piece my life back together
with undeterred determination
knowing tomorrow looms
awaiting my decision
though I'm still recovering from your rejection.

CONFESSION

Heavenly father, please help me to overcome this rejection. In the name of Jesus, I renounce the spirit of rejection. I break and destroy completely the stronghold of rejection. Lord, help me to remember that I am not alone but You are with me as I go through this very low period of my life. I thank You that You have made a way for me to be free from rejection and to learn to live as Your child. I commit everything into your hand, please lift me up above every form of rejection in the name of Jesus (Psalm 27:10)

THE WORD

Proverbs 12:25
Worry weighs a person down; an encouraging word cheers a person up...

Chapter 3

Failure

It's the desire of every woman to be successful. I have never met anyone who purposely set out to be a failure. But failures will come and when they do they hurt deeply and can be catastrophic. They bring feelings of defeat, hopelessness, destruction and despair. Their effects can be long-lasting, leaving marks in our hearts, tricking our minds into believing things that aren't true, distorting our perceptions of our goals and making them seem unattainable. Failures often create mental hurdles that can be difficult to overcome in many years to come

Proverbs 24:16
The godly may trip seven times, but they will get up again.

FALLING SHORT

Generous, virtuous
hardworking, loving
noble, stable
joyful, soulful
successful
diligent, confident
wise, nice
blessed with
happiness
creative, productive
strong, the virtuous one
depicted in Proverbs 31.

The church said I must be like her
this paragon of a woman
painted to be the epitomeof the perfect one.

All other women pale in comparison to her
her influence reaches beyond...near and far.
But can I be like her
is that even possible?
is this woman for real
is she even relatable?

Up at the crack of dawn
working on her farm

had her own garden
reaping her own fruits and vegetables
running her business
very, very savvy
a wonderful homeowner
who seems genuinely happy.

Her husband praised her
children adored her
women ran to her
men spoke of her
She was the 'it'
very accomplished.

But, I'm nothing like her
I'm very, very sure
nothing in me for others to adore,
I'm just a simple girl
finding my space in this world
trying to stay afloat
without rocking the boat,
hoping, hoping
life will turn out right
for I won't give up without a fight.
and someday
maybe, just maybe
I can become a little like her
a Proverbs 31 kinda girl.

CONFESSION

Father, I have struggled for so long to believe the truth that I am worthy and priceless. Forgive me for the comparisons I make and the contempt I feel about myself. Help me to know that I am loved because you say so. I am forgiven, for you died on the cross for me. In Jesus' Name, Amen.

THE WORD

Psalm 139:14
Thank you for making me so wonderfully complex! Your workmanship is marvelous—how well I know it.

DESTINED TO FAIL

I was set up to fail
from the get-go
there was nothing I could achieve.
my mother told me so…
DailyI believed her
every word she said
and soon those words took root in my head.

They have affected
every single thing I'd do
every road I'd trod
every path I'd choose.
They followed me everywhere

caring not who was around
always, always crushing my plans to the ground.
it didn't matter what strategies I'd use
or how I held them tight
try as I might
they never, ever turned out right.

I've never tasted success
don't know what it feels like
yet, I long to be dazzled and someday share a limelight.
If I can only get rid of those words spoken to me
which have become a bedrock
and will ultimately
destroy my ability
to do more than merely exist
to soar, to fly
to explore infinite possibility.

So I have no plans
nowhere I want to be,
I accept life as is
struggling daily in my reality
embracing whatever is thrown at me.

Everyone thinks I'm worthless
that I will never amount to anything
they say life will pass me by
leaving me nothing.

except mouths to feed and men disappointing me
mountainous roads to climb
never a chance to smile.

Maybe they are right
maybe I'm what I was destined to be living a life of limited possibility
accepting that the here and now
is how it's supposed to be
that tomorrow holds no joy for me ,
words stuck in brain
my life will always be filled with failures and pain
maybe I'm just destined to fail.

CONFESSION

Lord Jesus, Proverbs 18:21 says "The words of the reckless pierce like swords, but the tongue of the wise brings healing." I renounce every negative word spoken over my life and has impaired my growth. I pray that Your words will bring healing to me. According to Proverbs 18:21 "Death and life are in the power of the tongue." Help me to speak life every day of my life. In Jesus name, Amen.

THE WORD

Proverbs 15:4
*Gentle words are a tree of life; a deceitful
tongue crushes the spirit.*

Chapter 4

Unmet Expectations

Most of us grew up with a visual picture of what we want our lives to look like. We create mental images in our minds of the perfect family, career, house, car, and lifestyle. We dream, aspire, imagine and project future goals and desires. For most of us life is not the mirror image of what we imagined and all we are left with are unfulfilled expectations, unmet needs, shattered dreams, enormous setbacks and colossal failures. Expectations and dreams are great but when dreams fail, they leave us confused, disillusioned and sometimes devastated. Unfulfilled, unmet expectations can be traumatic, tragic and heartrending especially if there seems to be no hope in sight.

THE WORD

Psalm 69:2
Deeper and deeper I sink into the mire; I can't find a foothold.
I am in deep water, and the floods overwhelm me.

UNPLANNED LIFE

You said we'd stay together, forever
and I believed you
Now I feel so stupid
as nothing you said was true.
You've lied from the very beginning
and I was so gullible
now
I'm totally alone, depressed and confused.

I should have said no, and held on to my dreams
should have heeded the warnings that were bursting at the seams.
should have listened when mom warned me about you
when she said you were insincere and egotistic too.
Dad told me to wait awhile but I did not listen
I felt my female intuition would prove them all wrong,
and me true.

This was not the life I had planned for myself
no skill,
no qualification,
no path to success.
a baby at the hip, needing to be fed
no ring on my finger, no promise to be wed.
just dashed dreams in ashes lay
reminders of my failures day after day.

I've failed, failed miserably
to live up to the greatness that was expected of me.
now I must get up
must find the strength to arise
despite all that's happened in my unplanned life.

CONFESSION

Lord Jesus, I am broken, confused and disappointed with my life. I confess that I have placed my happiness and wellbeing in the hands of others. Please forgive me. Your word in Jeremiah 29:11 reminds me that You have a plan for my life. Help me to know, accept and embrace what this plan is. Father, it is my desire to do the work that You called me to and to walk in the fullness of the plans that You have for my life.

THE WORD

Proverbs 19:21

You can make many plans but the Lord's purpose will prevail.

PRESCRIPTION LIFE

Why does life work this way
why can't it just stay
exactly how I planned
that it would be?

Why must life be a dichotomy
opposing forces
fighting for dominancy?

Why can't I just neatly compartmentalize my life
just as I had planned when I was just a little girl
looking to conquer the world? Then I could pursue
what I want
when I want
with whom I want
without affecting eternity.

For so long
I lived with dreams inside my heart
plans I never thought
could fall apart
plans I cherished
plans I nurtured
plans I made for the future
an internal blueprint
with success stamped
all over it.

Yes,
I had it all figured out
what my life was supposed to be
never thinking that reality
would one day intrude
causing a rude awakening
from my dream.

CONFESSION

Lord, my life has not turned out as planned. All my plans have gone awry and I have been living my life the way I see fit with no thought of You. I confess that I have had my own blueprint all of my life. I ask You to help me to slow down and to allow You to help me figure out which way to go and what to do. I need your help, I need Your strength, I need Your wisdom. In Jesus name…Amen

THE WORD

Proverbs 3: 5, 6

Trust in the LORD with all your heart; do not depend on your own understanding. Seek his will in all you do, and he will show you which path to take.

UNFULFILLED LIFE

sad
mad
unhappy
dejected
downhearted
miserable
inconsolable
crestfallen
heartbroken
sorrowful
mournful
that's how I feel today
a sea of emotions
tunneling my way
cascading over my soul
in boundless waves
trying hard to steal away
the niche I've carved
in my heart and soul.

Restless
listless
deliberative
pensive
regretful
remorseful

demotivated
hundreds of emotions threatening
to explode
this
engulfing
suffocating
low
slow
empty
lengthy
unfilled heart.

Nothing can console it
I'm losing it bit by bit
trying to make it settle
but little by little
that emptiness finds its way
inside
eating alive
who I am
so the search is on in earnest
to find me
to find solace
to find....God.

CONFESSION

Heavenly Father I confess that I feel empty and unfulfilled. I thank you for knowing my heart better than I do. I know you are able to bring my dead heart back to life through the power of the Holy Spirit. Renew my mind and give me confidence in the truth found in Your Word. Show me new ways and birth new dreams in me. Help me find my fulfillment in You first. In the name of Jesus Christ I pray, Amen.

THE WORD

John 10:10
The thief's purpose is to steal and kill and destroy. My purpose is to give them a rich and satisfying life.

UNCERTAINTY
(Single Parent)

Don't get me wrong
I'm a proud mom
I love my children
who are real life angels.
I adore them
without reservation
without condition
without hesitation.

They have my heart
each one has a space
their own special part.

But I never thought I'd do it alone
that I'd be forced to build a home
with no one to hold my hand
when things start going wrong.
With no one to celebrate
when the kids are doing great
when achievements are met
or when it's time to fret
and worry
when they do not hurry
to get home.

How will I make it work
with no financial assistance?
When doing it alone was never a part
of the original heart-to-heart?
The dollar can stretch
so much and no more
and having some support
would definitely help out
especially to feed hungry mouths
buy clothes or just fix a remote.

My Kids,
Will they understand
when there's no money?
when they're hungry
but there's no food to fill
the hole in their bellies? Will they get it
when there's only one pair of shoes
to traverse everywhere church, home, school, community
fair?
will they wear it with pride
keeping alive
the dream inside
that life will get better
easier
some day?

Now I battle my own insecurities
that my parenting skills are lacking
tenacity
consistency.
I take a hard look inside
as I realize
I need to change how I feel
though these emotions are real
for the sake of my children's happiness
I must accept that I'm doing this all by myself
with no help.

I wish I had someone with me
to hit the ground running
but I will be brave facing everything
that comes my way
every day
like a trouper
an overcomer
a strong woman.

They have no dad but that's ok
they will excel and achieve in every way
cause I will give my all for my sons
despite how difficult life may become
and when it's all said and done
I will make it as a single mom.

CONFESSION

Lord, help me to be both Mother and Father to my children. Keep me healthy and strong on those days when I am weak. Remind me to love them in the same way that you have shown that special love for me. Guide me with your Holy Spirit and give me the patience and compassion to love my children more deeply than I ever have.

Open my battered heart and lead me to comfort and peace. Please heal the pain I carry in my heart each day and close the distance between me and You. In Jesus name, Amen

THE WORD

Philippians 4:6-7

Don't worry about anything; instead, pray about everything. Tell God what you need and thank him for all He has done. Then you will experience God's peace, which exceeds anything we can understand. His peace will guard your hearts and minds as you live in Christ Jesus.

CHILDLESS

You can't explain the pain
The image of motherhood shattered
broken into tiny pieces
at my feet in heaps lay
appointment after appointment
disappointment after disappointment
the feeling of hopelessness
despair
failure
incompetence.

No one feels it
no one understands it
it's there though
it never leaves
it's
constant
rampant
daily

hourly
minute by minute
second by second.

The pain in my heart
is like nothing
I've ever experienced before
its excruciating
crushing
devastating
mind blowing
creating
hopelessness
bareness
reaffirming barrenness

I have nothing in my arms
nothing to hold
nothing to fold
nothing to console
no baby
no child
no cries
nothing but an
empty house
empty arms
empty bed
emptiness
childlessness.

CONFESSION

Father, this pain I feel is unbearable. It has always been my desire to bring forth a child, to feel him suckle at my breast. Lord I feel so useless, unfulfilled and barren. Help me Lord to trust You through this process. Show me the way You want me to go. Remind me daily that I am no less of a woman and help me to find joy as I seek to be submitted to Your will. In Jesus name, Amen.

THE WORD

Hebrews 11:11
It was by faith that even Sarah was able to have a child, though she was barren and was too old. She believed that God would keep His promise.

DEATH

I remember holding you in my arms
the day you were born
I fell in love with you instantly
loving you with every fibre of my being.

You have been my joy
my song
my salvation.
Now you're gone
and suddenly my life has stopped
I've ceased to live

nothing can fill this gap in my heart
every moment
everyday
every minute
every second
since death took you away.

I care about nothing nothing at all
everything is meaningless
everything seems wrong
I feel so cheated
when your life was snatched away
now I barely know the difference
between night and day.
Sleep is elusive
darkness is now my friend
it's a journey of utter confusion
which seems to have no end.

How can I go on? I am like a fallen leaf
will I ever survive this deep sorrow, this painful grief?
Will I ever again find a way to be strong?
Will I ever again enjoy life's sweet song?
Will I now live life all alone;yearning for the light which
around you shone?
Must I now live without your playful smiling face
That always took me when I'm sad to that serene, happy
place;
where nothing could go wrong and all would be right

How will I live without you in my life?
will I see your angelic face no more,
will I never hear you banging on my door?
will I not feel your pudgy lips in a kiss,
will I be left only to reminisce?
on those memories we lovingly create
in your very short time on this earth.
Now I'm alone
in the world vast and wide
how will I carry on?
without my baby girl by my side?

CONFESSION

Heavenly father, thank you that You are with me (Immanuel). Thank You for being with me now as I mourn the loss of _____. You are the God of all Comfort and I willingly receive Your comfort now. My heart is broken, my spirit is crushed, and I feel hopeless and so alone. Your Word says those who mourn will be comforted, help me to find peace and rest in You and in those around me who offer love and support. Where there is pain fill my heart with hope and joy which can only come from You. In Jesus name, amen.

THE WORD

Revelation 21:4 (NLT)
He will wipe every tear from their eyes, and there will be no more death or sorrow or crying or pain. All these things are gone forever."

Chapter 5

Confusion

Let's face it we all get confused at times. Each of us at some point in our lives, is faced with confusing and disturbing thoughts leading to stress and anxiety. These sometimes create a whole host of draining emotions which sometimes initiate prolonged periods of confusion causing us to feel as if we are stuck in a never-ending, foggy web of uncertainty and powerlessness.

Psalm 42:3
Day and night I have only tears for food.....

FINDING JESUS IN THE GREY

This morning
I sit in church but my mind is far away
bombarded by many things
focus deserts me today.
The service is rich,
Praises rising
blessings flowing,
but try as I might,
I can't keep my thoughts from roaming.

I look all around
everyone is moving
hands extending, worshippers dancing,
the atmosphere is electric,
the presence of God is here,
but my mind won't cooperate,
its roaming everywhere.

I try to play the part
pry my lips apart but deep inside I knew
it wasn't from the heart,
for today my heart is empty,
devoid of any feeling at all,
and though I know God is here
I cannot hear His call.
I so wish I could feel Him

through the maze of endless fears
that has my heart beaten
bogged down with despair,
that has my hands glued
stuck to my side,
refusing to be lifted
they do not yet realize
that God is here
and waiting for my praise.

Forcibly I decide to stop
fighting how I feel
I bow my head in prayer
and quietly accept defeat.
The tears begin to flow
as I let it all out
and before I know it
I begin to shout.

I then realize how very, very good
God has been to me
even in my down times
He shows up miraculously,
how He cares for me
each and every day
and never a thought to renege
when I go astray.
so, today I accede

God is not always black and white,
He knows as His children
we won't always be free and light,
Sometimes there are shades of grey
milling all around,
but even in those moments
God's presence can be found.

All He expects is our honesty,
to tell Him how we really feel
about the confusions that are
oh so very, very real
its knowing Jesus is truly never, ever far away,
And we can sometimes
find Him
in the
patches of grey.

CONFESSION

Lord Jesus, sometimes my heart is cluttered and crowded with so many things and I can't see You. Sometimes I feel so very far from You, so devoid of Your presence. Help me in those moments to accept by faith that You are here, right beside me, always. In Jesus name, Amen.

THE WORD

Job 10:15
….. If I am guilty, too bad for me; and even if I'm innocent, I can't hold my head high, because I am filled with shame and misery.

DROWNING

I try to drown myself in distractions
willing the days away.
hoping my emotions
will stay unaffected today.
I want to forget all the sorrows
that stifle dreams of tomorrow
afraid to face all my fears
that daily surround me.

My head is sometimes so heavy,
It keeps bowing down to the ground
sometimes hiding the tears
streaming to my mouth
travelling down to my throat
engulfing my body
erupting in never-ending sobs.

I try to silence the voices in my head,
telling me
I'm better off dead.

My insecurities are killing me.
am I truly a disgrace to my family?
Am I not worthy of living?
of breathing
existing?
now I'm just......drowning.

CONFESSION

Lord, today I feel beaten, so tired, weary and discouraged. I see no way out and I feel as if my only recourse is to give up totally. Things seem so gloomy. Nothing is going my way. Uplift my Spirit, oh Lord. Give me peace, give me joy. Give me happiness. I need hope. You alone can turn this around. Help my unbelief and rescue me I pray. Control my mind and strengthen my heart so I can have the confidence to tackle every issue that comes my way. Where I am weak make me strong. Where I am fearful grant me faith to believe that my situation can and will change if I trust You. In Jesus name, Amen.

THE WORD

Job 10:15
*If I am guilty, too bad for me; and even if I'm innocent,
I can't hold my head high, because I am filled
with shame and misery.*

SLEEPLESSNESS

Body aching
head spinning
the
world is upside-down
tossing, turning
counting, recounting sheep.
Sleep just won't come.
I close my eyes
but it has disappeared
vanished into thin air.

Sleeplessness
has become my recent companion
my trusted friend
days, weeks, months on end.

Locked in a dreamless haze
a sleepless maze
peace is forgotten
rest misplaced
replaced by stress.

I lay in my bed
adrenaline pumping
heart vibrating
My body

Filled with energy not needed
at night crazy thoughts flooding my head
filling my heart with fear and dread
flooding it
with a million tiny molecules
of things gone awry
keeping me up at nightwatching,
pacing, waiting for the light.

Insomnia manipulating my head
with scenes
strange themes
crazy thoughts
invading my heart
nudging sleep away
willing it to stay
in obscurity.

Days have become unfriendly an enemy of the body
a fusion of calamity
sleepiness
listlessness
instability
anxiety
low energy
much lethargy
irritability
irascibility

> depression
> frustration
> separation from reality.
>
> Now I'm just tired.

CONFESSION

Lord, the darkness that surrounds me is more than I can bear. I can't find my way anymore, I feel lost and desperate especially during the night. I can't sleep at nights and during the day I am barely able to cope with what I need to do. Heavenly Father, I pray that as I go to bed tonight that You would give me a peaceful night's sleep and help me to wake refreshed, ready and willing to do Your will. Thank you for Your promises that You will lift us out of this pit, that You know the plans You have for us to give us a future and a hope.

THE WORD

Proverbs 3:23-24

*They keep you safe on your way, and your
feet will not stumble. You can go to bed without fear;
you will lie down and sleep soundly.*

Chapter 6

Bondage

Bondage is dangerous. It causes us to stop sensing the presence of God making us feel empty, and dry. It takes away our purpose in life so we wander from one thing to another, no goals, no vision and no clear path in life. Bondage always reminds us of the times we mess up and fail. It undermines our self-confidence leaving us feeling like abject failures.

Bondage steals our identity, anointing, vision, authority and confidence, making us feel inadequate, overwhelmed, empty, intimidated, confused and blind to God and His purpose for our lives.

2 Timothy 2:26
*Then they will come to their senses and escape
from the devil's trap. For they have been held captive
by him to do whatever he wants.*

PRISONER IN MY HOME

I've become a prisoner in this lonesome place
confined daily to this static space,
broken by you day after day
knowing my life is just wasting away.
I'm like a caged bird with broken wings
untapped potential wasted dreams.

I've sold my soul for material things
latest fashion, expensive blings,
driving nice cars, living really high
though bit by bit I had started to die.
now, nothing here makes me as happy as I use to be
they've all lost the attraction they once held to me.

But, you, you control me, every inch of me
my soul, my mind, my body
you won't let me go, though you don't really want me
your sadistic mind just wants to destroy me emotionally,
you want to see me die slowly and painfully
so you've made me a prisoner behind lock and key.

Now, as I stare at the dull grey walls
I can't stop the tears as they freely fall,
I'm just hoping that one day I'll break free
and become the woman I was destined to be,
not a shell of a human, timid and afraid

but a strong one, bold, fearless and brave,
then I will be strong enough to launch out on my own
and not allow you to make me......a prisoner in my home.

CONFESSION

Lord, forgive me for placing material things before You. Help me Lord to lay up for myself treasures in heaven. It is Your will that I do not lay up material treasures on earth for myself, where moth and rust can destroy and where thieves can break in and steal. Your Word states that our lives do not consist in the abundance of the things we possess. Remind me oh Lord that where my treasure is, there my heart will be also. In Jesus' name, Amen.

THE WORD

Luke 12:21
A person is a fool to store up earthly wealth but not have a rich relationship with God.

STRIPPED

This is it
you've taken it all
I have nothing left to give
I'm just waiting for the fall.

You've stripped me,
layer by layer

leaving me naked, without an ounce of barrier
you've laid me bare for all to see
the power you have yielded over me.

It started subtly
a harsh word, a simple put down
an angry retort, a fleeting frown
then it was displeasure with everything I do
nothing made you happy and nothing appeased you.
but now it has grown
making you someone unknown
and like a volcano
threatening to erupt
and it's way too much, it's overflowing my cup

Now everything I do
is a problem to you.
Wearing too much makeup
or putting none on my face
wearing a simple sandal
or a sneaker without its lace.
My hair, my clothes
my face, my nose
my hands, my feet
the way I eat
the way I keep
the house
and now a sheet.
A sheet!

that takes the cake
cause it makes no sense at all
that you would get so angry
at where the sheet on the bed falls.

I should have left you a long, long time ago
but I was so certain you would grow that you would
eventually mature
become much more like my Boaz
instead you have become more controlling
more possessive
more vindictive
making my life a hell
with all
your misgivings.
You have taken so much of me
refused to let me be
anything of value to anyone else
not realizing you're also hurting yourself.

Now I'm like that caged bird
dying to be free
hoping you'll just go and leave me be
so I can rediscover
the 'me' I lost
in trying to please you
the me I lost
in the rubble of untruths

    the me I lost
   in your ruinous words
   the me you tore to pieces
    leaving me defeated
     the me you stripped.

CONFESSION

Lord, my heart is so heavy this morning. My sorrow is so great. Psalm 34:18 states that the Lord is near to the brokenhearted. I am thankful that I do not have to hold it all together or be strong for everyone in my life. You are my strength. Fill me with the peace and joy I know can only come from You during this hard time. Help me, Lord! Thank you, God, that you are close when I am hurting. Thank you God, for the comfort, grace and joy that only you can give. In Jesus name I pray, Amen

THE WORD

Psalm 147:3
He heals the brokenhearted and bandages their wounds.

Chapter 7

Brokenness

Life is not without tribulation and trials; we will all face difficult and painful circumstances. These situations can come in many forms; death, heartbreak, broken relationships, financial crises, illnesses. These can hit us out of nowhere and leave us feeling afraid, broken, crushed and alone.

Psalm 69:20

*Their insults have broken my heart,
and I am in despair. If only one person would
show some pity; if only one would turn and comfort me.*

BROKEN

Big dreams
made when I was just a little girl,
amazing dreams
to conquer the world.
Dreams made through the eyes of
an innocent child,
aiming to climb the corporate ladder
aiming for the sky.

You were my knight when you entered my world
filling me with promises
fantasies
securities
things craved by gullible girls.

But you took everything from me
and gave me nothing in return
you took my dreams
and each one you burned
still you would not stop
you wanted my mind and soul
under the pretense that you would make me whole.

Now you have me
exactly where you want me
totally dependent on you

bound by chains of your half-truths
the iron links keep me tied to you.

You own me
inch by inch
yet each time you touch me
my cells vibrate cause my body hates
the 'me' you have turned me into
almost a slave, totally reliant on you.

You break me
day after day
and I see no hope of
ever getting away.

I never envisioned
my life would turn out like this
I never planned for all the
opportunities I've missed.
I wish I could turn back the
hands of time
reclaim my dreams
and make them totally mine.
I wish I had the will power
to stand up to you
to never put up with
the hurtful things you do.
I wish I never believed the lies

> woven
> never allowed my dreams,
> my plans, my promises to myself
> to be broken by you.

CONFESSION

Father, I confess that I am emotionally worn out. Everything has been taken from me, my pride, my mind, my dignity. By believing his lies I have allowed the enemy to strip me. I bring my brokenness and give it to You. Help me to see that You are my God in this moment. Help me to see You as my Father, My friend, My confidante, and my support. Heal my broken, fragmented heart. In Jesus Name, Amen.

THE WORD

Psalms 31:12, 14-15

*I am ignored as if I were dead,
as if I were a broken pot……. But I am trusting you,
O Lord, saying, "You are my God!"
My future is in your hands. Rescue me from those
who hunt me down relentlessly.*

BROKEN DREAMS

I had great dreams
and I fed them very well
always kept them in the forefront
always to them tell
how we'd make it to the top
how we'd never, ever stop
climbing, climbing, climbing
until we make it.

Then one day my dreams shattered
every one of them
they laid on the ground in pieces
too tiny for attempts to mend so I spent hours
crying
waiting
debating
where to go from here
where once my dreams laid
a place now inhabited by fears.

Life's on hold now
frozen in time
the outlook is cloudy
like these dreams of mine.
There's no need to hurry
I'm going nowhere fast

the future holds no promise
nothing seems to last.

I have no destination
no place of rest
I feel so tired
filled with emptiness.
So my dreams lay in pieces with nowhere to go
For they had died that day
many years ago

PRAYER

Father, I confess that I am tired, I am weak, I am worn. I am at my wits end, at the very bottom of the ladder. My dreams are dashed, shredded, crushed. Lord, you alone can move my heart in a new direction that will bring me the peace and happiness I have always longed for. It may look different from what I envisioned but Your vision is greater than mine. You see the whole picture, I only see part. You know what will make me happy. Fill me with Your joy Lord. In Jesus' name. Amen

THE WORD

Proverbs 15:22
Plans go wrong for lack of advice; many advisers bring success.

CRUSHED

You sat and watched me bleeding
from the torture and torment of your beating
curled like a fetus
shivering at your feet
barely even conscious
bidding death to come
to release me
from
the pain
from the shame
from this senseless game
I'm forced to play
knowing there is no way
to ever win
and no way out.

You never cared what I was feeling
you laughed as I found myself reeling
from the brutal force of your hands across my face
the kicks
the hits
the threats
the public disgrace.
My fate it seems is already sealed
life for me no longer feels real.

How could I have loved you?
How could I have made do

with the crumbs you offer me
knowing nothing about this was real.
You laugh as I cried
you said no one cared if I died
you tormented me day and night
with no respite
You think it's all funny
though your child grows in my tummy.
still you find ways to cause me pain
you are evil and insane.

But it will be over soon
and you
you...........will burn in hell

CONFESSION

Abba Father, I'm hurting physically, spiritually and emotionally. The trauma I am going through is real and painful. Bind up my wounds Lord. Renew me. Wash my mind clean of the words and thoughts that are a lie from the enemy. Put every shattered piece of my broken heart back together and heal every scar left from this trauma. Show me what to do in this situation, where to go and who to go to. Lead me to the right counselor, pastor or church that will help me in the process of restoration. Thank you for guiding me through this process. I ask that the memories associated with this wounding and trauma be erased. Help my husband to understand and accept that what he is doing is evil and wrong. May you deal with him so that he will never hurt anyone again. in Jesus Name, Amen

THE WORD

John 10:10
The thief's purpose is to steal and kill and destroy.
My purpose is to give them a rich and satisfying life.

DAMAGED

The tears fall, running down my nose
representing who I am - a marred, broken rose
hiding away from the glare of the world
hoping no one discovers this broken, damaged girl
then they'll know it's all a sham
I project a lie, but I'm a far cry
from the success, I wish I possessed
I am a total failure.

I always seemed to have it together
so no one suspected that I was quickly crumbling
becoming a human wreck.
I had them all fooled
though alone I'd bemoan that my spirit was badly torn,
broken, like a
crushed stone.

I feel like that forgotten child
running blind
running wild.
my life is disintegrating

right before my eyes,
I can't seem to stop it from
spiraling out of control
the failures won't stop, they seem on a roll.

So,
with pain in my eyes
I'm trying to lose my disguise
with my heart breaking open
I'm trying to do more than just coping
trying to lose all this hate
the anger and hurt that vibrates
through my body and soul
making me old,
broken and damaged.

CONFESSION

Abba Father, You are the Healer of the brokenhearted. You declare that You bind up their wounds. Because You are the healer, please heal all my emotional wounds. By Your love and power, remove the hurt and anger that I am experiencing. Help me to move on to emotional wholeness according to Psalm 147:3 which says, 'He heals the brokenhearted and binds up their wounds.'

THE WORD

Psalm 51:17
The sacrifice you desire is a broken spirit. You will not reject a broken and repentant heart, O God.

Chapter 8

Insecurities

Insecurity is a struggle that many of us can relate to. The "you're-not-good-enough" message has affected many of us in one way or another. We constantly struggle with society's standards and expectations; we feel pressured to lose or gain weight, change the colour of our skin, or "fix" the shape and contours of our bodies. Social media has evolved and has become the standard by which we measure ourselves and our lives, causing us to salivate for and compare ourselves with other women who seem to have perfect lives - the perfect body, the perfect status, the perfect relationship, the perfect career. As a result, we become discontented with who we are and what we have been blessed with. We begin to feel that we are never enough - never pretty enough, never strong enough, never smart enough, just never good enough in general.

No matter what kind of insecurity we may be facing, God wants us to walk in the freedom and truth of His Word. He desires for us to find peace and contentment in Him. He wants us to know that He loves us, He made us beautiful and He created us for a purpose that He will help us to complete.

Psalm 139:14
Thank you for making me so wonderfully complex!
Your workmanship is marvelous—how well I know it.

FALSE SECURITY

There's a false sense of security
that exists inside each of us.
A false sense of belief
that everything hinges
on our accomplishments.
The belief that,
we should trust
in the life we have carved for ourselves.
the accumulation of
things we possess.

We gather and hoard
and take onboard
all the worldly possessions we can,
all the glitz and glamour
that make us the envy of every 'woman.'

LOOSE TO LIVE

we glory in our stuff
all the material fluff
we can't seem to get enough.
Fancy homes,
extravagant cars
our ability to travel near and far.
We begin to trust
in the overabundance of possessions,
in our accumulations
money
jewelry
clothes
stocks and bonds.

So,
we boast
we gloat
we flaunt
the proliferation of all these things
the satisfaction and joy they appear to bring.

We allow the stuff we possess,
to define who we are
not understanding that there's a greater call
to put our trust in someone else
someone far above our possessions and wealth
to ensure our souls are secured
and we stand ready to live and reign with
Christ forevermore.

CONFESSION

Father, I confess that I have placed my trust in the earthly things I possess. I have developed and live with a false sense of security. Lord, help me break free from the voice of the enemy and embrace Your truth. Help me listen and know that I am loved, that I am perfectly made, and that I am accepted as I am in You. Please forgive me for allowing earthly possessions to dictate my thoughts, actions, words, desires, and motives. Help me to cleave to Your truth and reject the lies of the enemy. In Jesus' name, amen.

THE WORD

Matthew 6:21
*Wherever your treasure is,
there the desires of your heart will also be.*

INSECURITIES

Today I know you love me
tomorrow I don't
constant affirmations
is what my life is about.
I'm never, ever content
with where I am right now
I'm always bracing for the worst
always planning a way out.

Try as I might to be reassured
uncertainty takes root

LOOSE TO LIVE

planting thoughts, sometimes so obscure
my mind keeps reeling
messing up my feelings.
So I've built walls of insecurities
walls meant to keep me safe,
no is one allowed to cross
for my control would be the lost
if my walls were ever broken…down
or,
if I'm needed no more.

I never mean to put up my guard
but I can't help it sometimes
I don't want to be hurt
when people start crossing the line.
so I refuse to let anyone close
I keep pushing them away
I may seem heartless and cold
but it's only because I'm afraid

My insecurities protect me
they are my daily shield
from all the hurts and pains
that everyday I see
but I do hope…one day
I can put my insecurities away
and just let myself be
safe, secure and free in my love for Me.

CONFESSION

Loving Father, I confess my feelings of insecurity and inadequacy to You. I ask You to help me break free from this subtle but deadly bondage. I confess that I've listened to the voice of the enemy more than I've listened to your truth. Please forgive me and help me listen and know that I am loved, that I am perfectly made, that I am accepted as I am in You. Give me your Spirit to help me see when I am listening to lies instead of truth. Help me fix my eyes on You and all You are and have done for me and for this world. Thank you Lord! In Jesus' name I pray, Amen.

THE WORD

John 14:27
I am leaving you with a gift—peace of mind and heart.
And the peace I give is a gift the world cannot give.
So don't be troubled or afraid.

SOMETIMES

Sometimes,
sleep won't come
the pain seems unbearable
anxiety attacks the soul
as pain takes its toll.

Sometimes,
tears come at unexpected times

knocking me over like an out of
control tide,
creating a Tsunami of unimaginable degree.

Sometimes
nights are hard
agony seems more acute in the dark
in the stillness
in the aloneness
and I don't know if I can make it another day.

Sometimes
I'm confused
frustrated
exhausted
longing for healing
from the stress
distress
every excruciating day.

Sometimes
there's a vacuum
in my soul
in my heart
in my mind
a hole
un-occupied
unfulfilled
empty.

A soul
searching
yearning
hoping
to be filled
by something
by everything?
success
wealth
Someone....
a soulmate?
a lover?
or maybe......God.

CONFESSION

Abba Father, I am anxious and worried about so many things today. Dear God, I know that You are with me in whatever I face. I confess my need for You and ask Your forgiveness in trying to figure everything on my own. Give me the ability to trust You more, give me a heart that finds rest in Your presence, give me the wisdom to seek peace and pursue it. Remind me that I do not have to walk in fear or live in overwhelmed cycles of worry and stress. In the Mighty Name of Jesus, Amen.

THE WORD

Proverbs 3:5-6

*Trust in the Lord with all your heart;
do not depend on your own understanding.
Seek his will in all you do,
and he will show you which path to take.*

Chapter 9

Aging

Getting older is a natural process designed by God. Yet aging brings with it many frightening realities – frail bodies more susceptible to illness, dwindling strength and energy, physical and emotional changes, feelings of uselessness and abandonment, the seeming imminence of one's own death, financial concerns due to dwindling income. Then there is the fear of loneliness which brings with it feelings of alienation from everyone……children, grandchildren, friends, church community.

Ecclesiastes 12:1

Don't let the excitement of youth cause you to forget your Creator. Honor him in your youth before you grow old and say, "Life is not pleasant anymore."

GROWING OLD....ALONE

I know there's sadness in my eyes
as slowly I realize
that I'm in the fight of my life
trying to slow down the hands of time
which just seem to be speeding away
rapidly merging night and day.
It's hard to tell the difference
when it's going so fast
and nothing seems to last
except maybe,
yesterday and its memories.

Today is no different
time refuses to slow down a bit
putting me in a fit
as my age seems to be competing
with it.
Can't believe I'm this old
I'm not prepared at all,
slow down
slow down
is my daily call.
but,
it's not listening.

LOOSE TO LIVE

It's clear I'm beginning to age
my body is showing signs of wear and tear,
and the energy I now possess is sure not the same
as it used to be
when I was
young and free.

I used to do things with so much ease
but now my entire body seems about to freeze
now little things trigger discomfort and pains,
and the quality of the things I do
are just not the same.
I'm beginning to get forgetful
failing memory is upon me,
I misplace things all the time
and can't seem to control my mind
this minute I know what I want
the next I scarcely have a clue
how to be assertive, strong and independent
in anything I do.

I try not to look in the mirror
try hard not to confirm what I see
but sometimes I catch a glimpse,
and can hardly recognize me.
So I spend all my days reminiscing
on who I used to be,
but what makes me really sad

is what people refuse to see,
that beneath my aging, worn out self
is still the same old me.

The one who was filled with life,
so much to give and say and do
the one who gave so much pleasure
at home
at church
in our little town too.

Now I'm beginning to ache.
and my heart once filled with joy,
is slowly starting to break.
Cause now that I'm getting older,
feeling lonely may be status quo,
but never did I envision
getting old
and being alone.

CONFESSION

Lord, I am so scared of getting old and being alone. Teach me to grow old with greater joy everyday. Protect me from aging with bitterness and remorse. Give me Your wisdom, courage and strength. Help me to find comfort in those You have place around me. Help me to never become so discouraged, depressed or disturbed so much that I fail to recognize You are always with me. In Jesus' name, Amen

THE WORD

Psalm 92:14
Even in old age they will still produce fruit;
they will remain vital and green.

WHEN THE GIRLS SAG

I'm not as attractive as I used to be
so he keeps telling me
I've lost all my beauty
that attracted him to me.
His verbal abuse is endless
ripping away my confidence
it has become more relentless
as my girls bow defenseless.

They are not as pert
or as hard as they used to be
they have become saggy
laced with elasticity,
so now he has a problem
and is really hurting me
though he knows I can't control
the aging of my body.

These breasts have done a lot
weathered many storms,
fed three tiny tots.

They never ever complained
even when they're enflamed
never ever cared when he brought them pain
with his kneading and his pinching
his caressing and his sucking
but now he's complaining
that they're just no good
they are hurting his pride and threatening his manhood.

I try to hide my hurt
I never let it show
but I'm really very saddened
I wish he would just go
and leave me with my battle scars
which will one day heal

I will continue to be strong
despite how he makes me feel
like a complete failure and an aging hag
simply because I'm growing into my twilight years
and the girls are starting to sag.

CONFESSION

Lord Jesus, I present my body to You now as a living sacrifice. I consecrate all the members of my body to Jesus Christ and to Him alone. I consecrate areas of my body that are aging and ask that You Lord teach me how to embrace each change. Help me not to allow anyone to dictate what 'great' looks likes. Remind me even as I age that I am fearfully and wonderfully made. I bring my body fully under Your rule and under Your dominion. My body belongs to You, Lord, and I consecrate it to You right now fully, totally, completely.

THE WORD

2 Corinthians 4:16

That is why we never give up. Though our bodies are dying, our spirits are[a] being renewed every day.

Chapter 10

Hiding

Many of us have fine-tuned the art of Hiding. We've developed and successfully don many masks and have been wearing them for months, possibly years. Masks that hide who we really are and project only what we want others to see. We have a well-behaved daughter mask, an upstanding christian girl mask, an anointing spirit-filled mask, an entrepreneurial mask, loving wife and doting mother masks, a 'I have it together' mask.

For many of us it has become exhausting keeping up every façade and ensuring our masks are always securely in place....but we have become dependent on them so we wear them anyway...... If we remove our masks, what would the world see? Insecurities, pride, shame, malicious thoughts, unhappiness, brokenness, pretension?

2 Corinthians 4:2

We reject all shameful deeds and underhanded methods.
We don't try to trick anyone or distort the word of God.
We tell the truth before God,
and all who are honest know this.

ALCOHOLISM

(Hiding Behind the Bottle)

I never intended to drink
to become an alcoholic
I never meant to become so addicted
that I can't exist without it.
I really intended to stop after that first drink
but I fell in love with the oblivion which dulls my ability to think.
Now slowly I drink my days away
hoping it would continue to dull the pain
hoping I'll never again
experience the deluge of the rain.

I promise myself each day
never to drink again.
never to use the bottle to masquerade my pain.
but I can't seem to stop now, it has become

my safety net
I can't say no so I'll live with all the regrets.
there is no way out, at least none I've seen yet.
and now I'm on the brink of destruction, desperation.....
death.

I really should quit
cause I'm way past my limit
I've lost all my earthly possessions
now I have nothing except what's in my hand.
My children are but strangers passing me by
with guarded looks and way too sad eyes.

I'm daring death each and every day
hoping it doesn't come my way.
but the bottle has become my friend
journeying with me to the end
it's there for me even when
everyone leaves even my dearest friends
who fail to believe I could ever be whole again.
Maybe it's true
there's nothing more to do but
continue hiding behind the bottle.

CONFESSION

Father, I confess that I become addicted to alcohol. I drink all the time Lord so much so that I can't function without it. But now my life is quickly spiraling out of control. Lord I know that I am not able to break free of this destructive habit and ask that in Your grace and mercy You would help me to be set free of this deadly addiction. I renounce my need to hide from reality, my need to drink myself out of oblivion. I renounce my addiction and my destructive behavior. Replace my sadness with your happiness, grace and peace. In Your name I pray, Amen

THE WORD

1 Peter 4:3
You have had enough in the past of the evil things that godless people enjoy—their immorality and lust, their feasting and drunkenness and wild parties, and their terrible worship of idols.

WEALTH
(Hiding Behind the Wealth)

A corporate woman by day
a shell of a woman by night
fighting deep dark demons
that stay hidden when there's light
they wait for the cover of
darkness
to make themselves known
knowing I'm alone in my vast dark home.

I hate when they come
they never stay hidden
they wreak endless chaos
in a soul badly beaten
A soul so empty, filled only with big, big holes
A soul dead to happiness, joy and even hope.

I never tell my story
no one would understand
all they see is a wealthy accomplished dame
many accolades to her name
well-dressed in my ornate chair
daring anyone to question my right to be here.
I've earned it all, there's no doubt
I've a right to be proud, even celebrate my clout
after all I've made sacrifices others only dream of
given up things others chased daily after

But, now I have it all
but who to share it with is the call
I have no one, I'm lonely and forgotten
I have only memories of things that could have happened
on my climb to success.
I'm filled with regrets
because all I have left
are the things I possess
things that now seem meaningless.
I would gladly give them away
if my life I could replay
if the decisions I made could be washed away
and in return I'd have a new day.

Then the abortions would be a distant memory
and the monsters in my soul
could no longer harm me
and I would enjoy, companionships, friendships
health
all these I would give in exchange for my wealth.

CONFESSION

Father, please forgive us for greed, selfish ambition, idolatry, conceit and arrogance. Forgive us for loving things and placing them over You. Forgive us for not being good stewards of Your blessings. I renounce any gods of materialism. In Jesus' name. Amen

THE WORD

Ecclesiastes 5:10
Those who love money will never have enough. How meaningless to think that wealth brings true happiness.

BEHIND THE MASK

I seem great, awesome, beautiful in every way
I'm envied as I live from day to day
I work, I laugh, I write, I sing,
I seem anxious for what each new day might bring.

Then I get home and remove my mask
now being happy seems an impossible task,
as the darkness in my soul rises to the fore
throwing all my happiness out the door.

I cry, I scream, I bawl, and sleep,
even though I have promises to keep.
I wait, and wonder, and cry some more,
And I ache and burn from my very core.

No one sees the smiles I fake,
the scars I wear
the tears I make
the thoughts of suicide
tormenting in my mind
holding me hostage

dulling my shine
clinging
cleaving
never giving up
refusing to leave.
Loneliness has become my best friend
frustrations and depressions
have no end.
Happiness is a lie
goals and plans are trapped in time
lost in consequences of opportunities denied
loving has gotten me nowhere,
my achievements are fueled by fear
a deep void occupies
my heart and mind.

My heart is weak,
my body feels dead
my passions are nonexistent
my soul is lead.
For nothing can make me feel again
I'm living the life of a human dead.

No one knows what I'm going through
I wear my mask very well
I give nothing away
no one my struggles I tell

but now I'm breaking
I'm tired of pretending I'm strong
I want to be vulnerable
I want to sometimes be wrong.

I want to get rid of this mask I designed
I want to be free
to laugh
to wear a genuine smile
to shed the false bravado.
I project to the world
I no more want to be
this insecure little girl.
all I want
all I ask for
is help
to unveil
to live beyond my mask.

CONFESSION

God, You call your followers to be honest. Honesty brings about transformation. And transformation ultimately results in peace. Unmask me so I can be free from the pain of pretense, be free to be who I truly am. A daughter of the King of Kings and the Lord of Lords. Unmask me Oh Lord so the world can see You in me daily. In Jesus Name, Amen

THE WORD

Matthew 23:28
Outwardly you look like righteous people, but inwardly your hearts are filled with hypocrisy and lawlessness

MASKED

There is a frail and fragile me
living behind this mask
laden with insecurities
feeling happiness is too much to ask
projecting always a ready smile
hiding years of deep turmoil
neatly buried beneath tons and tons of lies.

Concealed behind the mask
a heart frequently broken
chained with deep resentment
and anger unspoken.
Here my fear hides
here sadness resides
here truth unfolds
but only behind the tightly closed doors of my home
daily I was slowly dying.
I couldn't go on,
there was something missing

LOOSE TO LIVE

Behind this mask is where I cover my constant tears
shield my eyes from unwanted stares
hide my true reactions
feign fake expressions,
sometimes deep confusions
and intense rebellion.
Hoping no one can see
the vulnerable, wounded me,
the shattered dreams
the silent screams
the open putrefying wounds
my stolen buried youth
stolen by lies masquerading as truth.

But
behind the mask has become lonely
making me isolated and unfriendly
fearful
resentful
distrustful
untruthful
unable to breathe
as it closes in on meI feel trapped
behind this facade of phony smiles.
maybe it's time
to remove this mask of mine.

CONFESSION

Lord, today, I want to remove the mask I've been wearing for so long. I want to be accepted for who I am and not what others want me to be. I want to be who You want me to be. I repent of wearing this mask of deception and ask for Your forgiveness. Help me to see myself the way You see me and to walk the way You walk so I can lead others to You. Remove my fears of not being accepted and keep me strong when I'm tempted to grab the mask and hide behind it again. Help me to own up to my wrongdoing and to walk it through instead of wanting to run away from the problem. Thank you for always loving me for who I am even when I make mistakes. I ask this all in Jesus name…Amen.

THE WORD

2 Corinthians 11:14 (NLT)
But I am not surprised! Even Satan disguises himself as an angel of light.

SMILING THROUGH IT

I have a signature smile and I wear it all the time
it's always there, through the battles and the strife's
I never, ever lose it
it's my defense against the world
it keeps me strong and focused
and hides all my fears.

Life has been a maze, full of twist and turns
I've been battered and bruised
and sometimes badly burned
I've hit rock bottom many, many times
sometimes contemplating ending my sorrowful life
and it's been hard riding out the tides
but never have I lost my signature smile.

It's a facade I wear very well
always ensuring it's in place
no one cares to look beyond it
no one sees beyond the face
they all think I'm fine and all is going well
they know nothing of my pain
nor my secret hell,
so, each time I leave home even for a little while
I leave them all behind and don my signature smile.

I have everyone fooled
or so it would seem
but when I look in the mirror

I'm no longer surprised to see
clouded, dazed and dark eyes staring back at me
telling me my life is fake and it won't last
I must get rid of my defense
I must lose my mask.

Ignoring my problems won't make me emotionally fit
I can't go through life just smiling through it.

CONFESSION

Heavenly Father, in Jesus' name, please help me to dwell in Your secret place today. Help me to remain stable and fixed under Your shadow. Keep my emotions on an even keel today. Help me to just focus on You so that You can make me perfectly stable in every way. Help me to be sincere and honest in all I do. Forgive me for the secrets I've tried to keep hidden from You. Thank You, Father. In Jesus' name, amen."

THE WORD

Proverbs 26:23
Smooth[a] words may hide a wicked heart,
just as a pretty glaze covers a clay pot.

FAKING IT WHILE MAKING IT

To many I am a strong woman
phenomenal
independent
successful
suave
cocky
aggressive
intelligent
beautiful
sitting at the top of a male-driven world.

To many I am
selfish
self-centered
egotistical
disloyal
a class 'A' bitch
totally devoid of emotion
I seem to have it all
men desire me
women hate me
young girls want to be like me
husbands want to be unfaithful with me
bachelors want to date me
women want to befriend me
everyone wants something from me.

But they don't know
They don't know me
they know nothing of my
vulnerabilities
insecurities
loneliness
fears

They don't know
how I
cry myself to sleep at nights
surrounded by loneliness
yearning for companionship
that can only be found in the arms of a soulmate.

How the smile I wear hide deep dark secrets
deeply ingrained scars and bruises covered masterfully
by expertly applied blushes and rouges
How I masquerade a fragile sense of bravado
wearing my self- made defenses like a shield.

They don't know how I don my armor daily
ensuring every single piece is in its rightful place
Hoping that each day will be the day I stop
faking it while making it.

PRAYER

Heavenly Father, I come to You today, confessing that I have not lived my life the way that You would have wanted me to. I've faked so many areas of my life and I come to You in humility of spirit, knowing that in Your loving-kindness You forgive those that are of a contrite heart. Father, I want to turn my life around and live in a way that is transparent before You – a godly life that is pleasing to You and a life that brings glory to Your name. Cleanse my heart of sin. Give me a teachable heart so that I may live a godly life in Christ Jesus, knowing that this is Your will for my life. In Jesus name I pray, Amen

THE WORD

James 4:17
Remember, it is sin to know what you ought to do and then not do it.

Chapter 11

Loneliness

Loneliness is a major social problem in our modern society. Mother Teresa once said "the feeling of being unwanted is the most terrible form of poverty". She also described loneliness as the leprosy of the modern world. With all our advances, technological and otherwise, we all know what it's like to feel lonely, to be in a group and yet feel terribly alone. There is in all of us an insatiable need to be important to someone else, to be loved, to feel worthwhile.

Psalm 25:16
Turn to me and have mercy,
for I am alone and in deep distress.

EMPTINESS

I want to fill this empty space
that seems a hollowed pit
something is missing inside me
and nothing seems to fit.

I long to fill the emptiness
and satisfy the inner hunger
life has left me drained and starved
and in nothing I can find the answer.

Outside myself, I start to look
but still there stands the void.
The little things I used to love,
I no longer enjoy.

I try to talk to Jesus,
for I'm his and he is mine,
but even though I know him;
I'm still not feeling fine.

Tomorrow, I'll go searching,
and see what I find
hopefully I'll meet Jesus
to set free this heart of mine.

CONFESSION

Jehovah Jireh, the supplier of all my needs, I need You now. Today, I am weary, weak and drained. I feel so empty, Heavenly Father. I feel as though there is a missing piece in the puzzle of my life. Help me to find strength, peace and stability in You. Fill my emptiness with Your strength and mighty power, that I will rise up once again. In Jesus name, Amen.

THE WORD

Job 15:31-32

Let them no longer fool themselves by trusting in empty riches, for emptiness will be their only reward. They will be cut down in the prime of life; their branches will never again be green.

WHEN HE CHEATS

I would have understood
if you told me from the get-go
you have found a new lover
and you can't tell her no.
You've become intoxicated
by her beauty, her allure
she has you bewitched
an obsession you can't ignore.

Instead you lied
and lied

then lied some more
made up stories when I found
glaring evidence
shooting from your phone.
Pictures you claimed belong to
someone else
though I know that mark outlined visibly
on your leg.

You should have stopped while you were ahead
but instead
you had to wait until you were caught
with your pants down
now everyone knows who you really are
a cheating clown.
a wolf in sheep's clothes
pretending to be a man of stature.

You've hidden behind religion
way too long
now you're left to sing your own
sinful song
and though I hurt, I have a sweet relief
when I see you
crumbling at my feet
revenge is always very sweet
and I'm happy
to be separated from a husband who cheats.

CONFESSION

Heavenly Father, I hurt so bad. I feel so betrayed. I lift my husband up before You and pray for peace in his heart. Show him Your grace, Lord, and help him see his worth in Your eyes and Your plan. I pray that I can become a beacon of Your love and forgiveness, Father, and can maintain the strength and faith he needs from me. In Jesus' holy name, Amen.

THE WORD

Hebrews 4:15
This High Priest of ours understands our weaknesses, for he faced all of the same testing we do, yet he did not sin.

ADULTERY

I'm in love with a man
who is not my own
he has another family
he has another home
I like it when he's by my side
hate that we must run and hide
I want to break it off, but I can't
since he supplies all my needs and wants.

He doesn't love me of that I'm sure
but, I make him feel important, he says
I make him feel secure

I make up for what his marriage lacks
constant nagging, put downs, verbal attacks.
yet his love is reserved for his wife and kids
since I'm only his side chick
not the
one wearing his ring.
and though he goes home to his family
I'm the one who makes him excited,
the one who makes him happy.

So, we continue to be secret lovers
hoping no one finds out
not our children
not our pastor
not the wife in his house.
I know it's wrong
but I'm just not strong
so, I play along
pretending I'm happy and free
though deep inside I feel melancholy
insulted,
used and
abused.
One day he will end it all
and great and devastating will be my fall.

I know this relationship is not good for me
my children, my God nor my family
surviving on the scraps he offers me
trampling daily on my dignity.
I know I'm shortchanging myself
but I'm in so deep; I can't exist without his help
cause financially he provides great support
paying my bills, buying me thrills
and keeping me afloat.

This life we are living is morally wrong
but how do I stop singing this adulterous song?
I still need him.
Won't I miss him?
and though the pain is severe from wounds so deep
all the promises he makes yet fails to keep
though the lies were many, I'd still believe
when he promised me comfort, my burdens to relieve.
His words were wind but a lasting impression they made
stuck in my head, they just won't fade

One day I will find the strength to move on
until then I will just take what he's able to offer me
hoping he'll never know how I really feel
when he decides to let me go, to set me free.

CONFESSION

Father God I have sinned. I know what I am doing is wrong but I can't seem to help myself. I repent of my sin. Give me the strength to let go and sever the ties that have been formed. I have separated what You have joined together, please forgive me. Help me to forgive myself.

THE WORD

Psalm 51:1-12
Run from sexual sin! No other sin so clearly affects the body as this one does. For sexual immorality is a sin against your own body.

MARRIED...BUT IN THE DARK

Our wedding day was among
the most memorable of my life
then we were certain our marriage
would stand the test of time
that our future would be full of smiles
but now, you don't want me.

So
this farce of a marriage
is coming to an end
finally closing
decades of pretense
without a doubt
we are on our way out.

I do love you
but your attention started to shift
nothing prepared us or made us ready for this...
this shell
of a marriage.
Now I'm giving up putting an end to this farce
knowing I could never again willingly give it my all
never willing to accept my role as your wife….. in the dark

You share nothing with me,
nothing at all
not about the house, the accounts, not even the car.
You say I'm jealous and insecure
but that's because you do not possess
a loyal bone.
Your life is a mystery, a shrouded mystery for sure
nothing about our lives makes sense
so there's nothing to restore.

You tell me you love me, but
that can't possibly be true
since I know absolutely nothing,
nothing about you.

I never know where you are
never know what you do
never know if what you tell me
is ever really true.

You act as if I'm invisible
as if I don't exist
as if my disappearance
is your greatest wish.

You show no affection…none to me at all
wouldn't stretch out your hands
to catch me if I fall.
I'm locked in a life of loneliness and pain,
darkness and shame.
A place unseen,
a place with only shattered dreams.

So what's the use
living like this?

CONFESSION

Dear God, although marriage can be so great, there are times that I feel so isolated from _____. Whether tension has built up from an outside source or from the relationship itself, it hurts. Please help us. I feel alone. Please bring the warmth of relationships into my life. Please cover my thoughts with hope. Please send your love into my heart. Grant me Your forgiving power. In Jesus name, amen.

THE WORD

Deuteronomy 31:8
*Do not be afraid or discouraged,
for the Lord will personally go ahead of you. He will be with you; he will neither fail you nor abandon you."*

BROKEN PICKET FENCE
(Divorce)

You say you're going away
you can't afford to stay
you've met someone new
so we must part ways.
you say life has become unbearable
and too difficult right now
our situation grew untenable
always leading to a row.
so we must say goodbye
and stop living a lie
you say I must accept it even if inside I really want to die.

This was never in the plan
when I chose you as my husband
we were supposed to stay together
even through the stormy weather
our children were destined to grow
knowing we'd always there
always confident we would calm their fears
now it's all gone
where did we go wrong?

How do I pick up the pieces
how do I go on from here?
how do I get past these big, big towers of fears?

how do I recover, choosing my pain not to wear
how do I even get used to you not been here?
how do I begin to mend this broken heart
how do I explain to our kids why we had to part?

True, we've had our ups and down
massive arguments, leaving us with a frown
we'd get it back together, after we have calmed
maybe our violent words had caused irreparable harm.

So the journey of our lives is ending here today
for the papers I hold will never go away
there's nothing more to do, nothing more to say
nothing more to fight for, nothing to repay.
Now I must say goodbye to the life we had made
knowing tomorrow a new life must take its place,
it's hard to accept failure
hard to accept defeat
hard to believe my life will ever again be complete,
without you in it

Nevertheless, I will recover
I will become stronger
despite, the dashing of my dream
the crushing of my sense
the destruction of my 'white picket fence.'

CONFESSION

Lord Jesus, my heart is heavy as I am having to face a divorce I never wanted and feel not only alone, but such a failure in my marriage. Help me Lord. Give me the strength and the courage to face this sadness in my life, keep me Lord from bitterness and may I face the proceedings with calm dignity and not bitterness or hostility. There is much pain in my heart, Lord. I pray that You will keep me from nursing any wounds and emerge from this ordeal closer to You. Thank You that You have promised to be with me through all the storms of life – and lead me in the path that You have planned for me, I pray, in Jesus name

THE WORD

Isaiah 43:4

*Others were given in exchange for you.
I traded their lives for yours because you are precious to me.
You are honored, and I love you.*

Chapter 12

Unhealthy Emotions

Satan often attacks us through our emotions. We can be doing the right things and embracing the correct beliefs and still fall prey to the tricks of the enemy through feelings that tempt us to sin: depression, discouragement, fears, doubts, unhealthy thought patterns and behaviors that dig trenches in our souls and wreak havoc in our lives.

Proverbs 15:13

A glad heart makes a happy face;
a broken heart crushes the spirit.

DEPRESSION

"You're not depressed " they say
"you're just lazing away your days
refusing to leave your bed
blaming what's inside your head
but you've been fed
by the lies you tell yourself everyday."

"You need to get it together" they say
"let today be the last day
you lay in that bed
pretending your life's a living hell
when you're living very well
better than most of us
yet we never make a fuss
about our lot in life."

But they don't know there's a war in my head
plunging me into darkness
without a thought about how I feel
about what's real.
They know nothing of the empty feeling
that comes from within
that tells me my life means nothing….absolutely nothing.

Real or perceived
that's how doubts are conceived

and then Poof! I'm losing control
of reality
Can I even control my sanity?

They don't know how I long to share my feelings
but always fearing that no one will listen
how I long to reach out with outstretched arms
but hesitating lest I find no one there.

I pick up the phone, but who to call
I feel overwhelmed; my mind is about to fall
the flames spark inside my head igniting fear
My thoughts are suicidal, I feel no one cares
emotional fires are lighting up my head
I feel drained, dry, distant, dead.
Consumed in my own darkness, I'm slowly fading away
my once blue and sunny sky have turned to clouds of grey
I see no hope of a better day
so why not end it all, right now, today?
and embrace peace...finally.

CONFESSION

Loving Father, I need You. I am suffering from depression and anxiety disorder. Give me the courage and strength to trust you and allow the Holy Spirit to guide me on where to seek help. Remind me that You love me and through your love all things are possible. Thank you that you never change, even when every-

thing around me is changing and unpredictable. (Hebrews 13:8) Thank you that you are stable, even when I feel so very unstable. Please sustain me, protect me, and enable me to stand. (1 John 4:4; Psalm 28:7) In Jesus' name I praise you. Amen

THE WORD

2 Thessalonians 3:16
Now may the Lord of peace himself give you his peace at all times and in every situation. The Lord be with you all.

INDECISION

I am just starting to get over you
now you reappear in my life
your lips dripping with lies
making me all confused
you say leaving was the biggest mistake
you ever made
you were selfish with the new life you intended to create.
Now, you want to come back into my life
to finally make me your wife.
you want me to wear your ring
and become your everything
you want to show the world I am the one
you're finally ready to stand up and be a man.

But something doesn't sit right
something is wrong with this life

you're attempting to create
hoping to entice me right back
with tales about fate
in spite
of how you treated me
as you left with your new mate.
Then I was all wrong
now I'm Mrs. Right
then you took my song
and almost took my life
when you told me I wasn't good enough
unworthy to be your wife.

what has changed between then and now?
that you're suddenly ready to make this serious vow
you tried so desperately to step aside
you seemed compelled to run and hide.
Do I want to take the chance
that what you said is true?
Do I still believe that I'm meant
to be only for you?
That you are my soul mate
and together we are a team
that I was created for you
and you were created for me?
that leaving me will not come to your mind again
that I can once again trust you and
allow you to be my best friend?

I just don't know what to do right now
but I'm scared to refuse
this offer of love though I'm really confused.

CONFESSION

Father, in the midst of my own uncertainty and confusion, I bow my heart, my will and my mind to you. Jesus, you know my heart better than I do. Father, cover me with Your love and Your calm me in my confusion. Stabilize my mind and grant me clear mind to make good, healthy decisions in my life. May the storms of my life cause me to cling more tightly to the truth of Your faithfulness, Your providence and Your sovereign care for me. In Jesus name, Amen.

THE WORD

1 Corinthians 14:33
*For God is not a God of disorder but of peace,
as in all the meetings of God's holy people.*

SADNESS

This pain I'm feeling
has me reeling
twisted in a tight knot
tightly wrapped
unable to react
to the pain of you leaving

me alone
in our home
which was once a serene place of rest
laughter and delightful sounds of happiness.

Now the house is empty
and silence permeates each room
there is no sound of your voice
that loud melodious boom.
I will hear your laughter no more
as you tickle me against the kitchen door
taunting me with silly kisses
that would make me weak
without ever missing a beat.

I must forget the happiness we once shared
the thousand ways you showed me you cared
the little things you would randomly do for me
making me gleeful with your spontaneity
how with one smile you could send shivers down my
sharing your thoughts without speaking a single line
proving our compatibility
was your daily reality as we built life from nothing
yet knowing we had everything

But,
it's all over
it's time to move on

now you're making life with a woman brand new
leaving me alone and dejected in your rear view.
I must rise from the ashes
without hesitation
piece my life back together
with undeterred determination
for I know tomorrow looms
awaiting my decision
though I'm still recovering
from your unexpected rejection.

PRAYER

Heavenly father, I come before you today, please help me to overcome rejection in the name of Jesus (Isa 41:13). Lord, help me to remember that I am not alone but You are with me as I go through this very low period of my life. I commit everything into Your hand, please lift me up above every form of rejection in the name of Jesus (Psalm 27:10)

THE WORD

Proverbs 12:25
Anxiety weighs down the heart,
but a kind word cheers it up.

Chapter 13

Victimization

Many of us have been exposed to traumatic events at some point in our lives, some more devastating than others. Some women come out unscathed but many continue to reel from these events even as adults. Being a victim whether sexual, physical or verbal creates vulnerability and a sense of powerlessness. It sometimes reduces us and creates passive, weak, deficient, fragile women filled with shame. It undermines our capacity to not only survive but thrive and flourish after adverse situations in our lives. It affects how as women we view ourselves and ultimately how we allow ourselves to be treated by others.

Psalm 34:17
*The Lord hears his people when they call to him for help.
He rescues them from all their troubles.*

ABUSED

I stayed with you for far too long
when all you did was treat me wrong
there were red flags
but I ignored the warning signs
for I feared being alone
I discarded wise guidelines.
So I killed what feelings I had left
hoping to someday to earn your respect.
But that day never came
and it was always the same
the cursing
the beatings
the bruises and scars
broken hand, broken rib, broken teeth and jaws
promises that you're going to change
but change never came
every so often you'd repeat the sequence
everything remained the same.

Still I loved, served and catered to you
fear became my motivation for everything I do
I lost my mind
I lost my voice
I lost myself
I'd wake up every day in my own private hell.
Still I stayed

day after day
I was too ashamed to explain
what my life had become
a cycle of beatings, cursing and endless abuse
a life that was no life at all
but apparently endless fun
to you.

Though you used, abused, and hit me hard
admitting you never loved me is a start
to healing the deep wounds of my broken heart.
The scars you leave, will fade and one day disappear
and new hopes, dreams and desires will begin to bear fruit.
until then I must find the courage or I will lose
my dignity my life underneath your abuse.

CONFESSION

Heavenly father, I know you love me. I hate what I've become, a punching bag, a mind filled with dirty derogatory words. Give me the strength to leave this situation before He takes my life. Help me to reach out to someone who is able to help me. Today I trade my sorrow, pains, hurts, shame for the joy of the Lord. I know it will take time but heal my broken heart, in Jesus' mighty name, Amen.

THE WORD

1 Peter 5:10
*In his kindness God called you to share in his
eternal glory by means of Christ Jesus. So after you have
suffered a little while, he will restore, support, and strengthen
you, and he will place you on a firm foundation.*

RAPED

He touched me
I hated it
groping, searching hands
invasive, intrusive, hurtful hands
skimming my untouched, unsoiled body
breaking my dreams, my aspirations....my innocence
my belief in humanity.

He touched me
I hated him
he revolted me
sickened me
made me fearful
weak
timid
broken
uncertain of life
uncertain of my future

Then one night
he did the unthinkable
he raped me
tore my hymen
tore my heart
tore my dreams
stripped me of my ability to ever 'be'
to ever view life through a child's eyes.

Many years have passed
but still.....
I remember it like yesterday
how dirty I felt
how much I wanted to die
How I hated him......
How I died that night
..... died a slow gut-wrenching death
In just one night he took it all

CONFESSION

Heavenly Father help me overcome my fear. Empower me with Your Word. Help to read it, pray it, memorize it, and speak it. Your words said, "who the son sets free is free indeed.' Set me free from this feeling of fear, dread, unworthiness, filthiness and anxiety. Please cleanse me of all defilement in the name of Jesus. I rebuke the spirit of rape and command that spirit to leave in the name of Jesus. Father God, I ask that the Holy Ghost now come and lift off all the pain and trauma and bring a complete healing in the name of Jesus, Amen.

THE WORD

Psalm 147:3
He heals the broken-hearted and bandages their wounds.

BLACK-SHEEP

Always called out
for the attributes I lacked
verbally attacked,
ridiculed for being different
treated like an outcast
taken for granted
my opinions, never counted,
my presence, unwanted
lost in a family
convinced I never measure up
to who they said I should be.

Growing
evolving
yet
always knowing
I was the black sheep

the title was mine to keep,
relegated to my own prison cell
my designated private hell,
in a family
that never wanted me
never could see
the beauty I could be
if anyone even cared.

Born to live,
yet yearning to die
tired of living a lie,
of hoping
that someday they would truly see 'me.'
Beautiful, talented
gifted…me
but… they never did see.
Sick and tired to the bone
I hereby surrender tired of fighting prejudice and
slander, slowly I'm accepting defeat
wanting to win but accepting I'm beat.
Rejected by my own
left all alone,
knowing I will never be
anything in this family
but the black sheep.

CONFESSION

Thank you that you see me right where I am, in the midst of my pain and struggles. Thank you that you have not forgotten me and You never will. I come before you today with a heart heavy with loneliness. I feel like there's no one who cares, no one with whom I can share the real me. I don't feel as if I belong anywhere. I don't feel connected to anyone. I feel like an outsider. Please help me Lord. I need you. In Jesus name, Amen

THE WORD

Psalm 27:10
*Even if my father and mother abandon me,
the Lord will hold me close.*

UTTERANCES OF DESTRUCTION

No scars
no bruises
no evidence for the world to see.
I never tell
it's my secret
my shame
my pain
to endure.

Like a recurring decimal
it comes everyday

A never-ending relay
of words
infused with anger
laced with hate
issued with malice
of unmanageable degree.

Never mind that I'm but a child
your child
your DNA runs through my vein
sand yet my hurt cause you no pains.
Your irrational behaviour makes no sense
how things could be just fine
laughter, merriment, jokes with punch lines
then,
poof!
without a single warning sign
rage!
intense ballooning into
a litany of lava-laced lines leap from your lips
searing me, shocking me
ripping me to strips

It takes awhile
for the tirade to end
but the fear engulfing me will never mend
I wish you would just hit me
with all of your might

then you'd get it out
the anger at my sight
then maybe we could move on
under the guise
that life is fine.

I don't understand its genesis
it just doesn't fit
something is clearly amiss
the stature of who you are
who you're perceived to be
doesn't match the reality
of the "you" known by me except with me
you're the like a demon
from hell.

CONFESSION,

Lord, I hate_____. He/she has and continue to break me down with words of hate, anger and malice. Lord forgive me. Teach me how to love _____ in spite of all he/she has done to me. Spread Your love in my heart to revive it because it feels dead. Help me Lord to believe what You tell me and dismiss the lies of _____. Help me now, I'm drowning. In Jesus name, Amen.

THE WORD

Ephesians 4:31-32

Get rid of all bitterness, rage, anger, harsh words, and slander, as well as all types of evil behavior. Instead, be kind to each other, tenderhearted, forgiving one another, just as God through Christ has forgiven you.

Chapter 14

Struggles

Struggles come in all shapes and sizes - fear, addiction, persecution, and worry. Whether we are 'old school' or millennial women we seem to be drowning under the weight of everything we have on our 'life plates' creating pain, disharmony, exhaustion, and a total disconnection with who we are. We struggle to hold it together, to live the balanced productive life. We bend and break ourselves, in an attempt to heal conflict and resolve challenges around us. We struggle – physically, mentally, emotionally and spiritually. We struggle with our many roles as mothers, providers, givers, servers which leave us lethargic, confused, and exhausted as we sacrifice sleep in order to 'get things done'.

Luke 10:41-42

*But the Lord said to her, "My dear Martha,
you are worried and upset over all these details!
There is only one thing worth being concerned about.
Mary has discovered it, and it will not be taken away from her*

JOBLESS

Sitting here, alone at home
wondering where to go from here
my life appears dark
hopelessness abounds everywhere.
Tried so hard to secure a job
efforts proved futile, I'm reduced to sobs,
I walk, I hitchhike, I run, I jog,
going from store to store
door to door
but with no luck
now I feel stuck
in this endless cycle
of failure and defeat.

I would have given up
a long, long time ago
except for that voice in my head telling me no
saying something will turn up
one of these days.
Keep striving, keep pushing,
victory is on its way.

But,
the days now seem to gallop away
still I search
still I seek
still I beg
still I speak
……still nothing.

So today I sit on a stone
my head overtaken with woes
wondering what to do with my life…
how to dull the noise
silent that other voice
that just won't let me becrowding my mind
all the time
telling me just to end my life
right here and now.

I try to pass the time
free my mind
I try not to listen to that voice
but it just won't go away
it wants to stay
in my subconscious
making me anxious
fueling hopelessness.

So I sit
hoping for a call
or even a text saying come clean my floor
or wash my clothes
or cook my dinner
or take my suits to the cleaner.
Right now I really don't care
bills are piling up everywhere.
I would do anything to earn a dollar
to care for myself, my kids and my mother.
to ensure they never again experience hunger
or the pressure
of a jobless daughter........a jobless mother.

CONFESSION

Dear Father in heaven, I need a job. Please help me to get a job for financial income, and the opportunities it would provide to use the talents you've given me to help make the world a better place. You know how hard I've tried to find a job. But so far, all the hard work I've done during my job search hasn't led to any job offers. I'm frustrated, my confidence has been shaken and I'm worried about my future. God, please send the miraculous breakthrough I need to get a new job soon. I believe that there are no limits to what you can do for me. In Jesus' name I pray, Amen.

THE WORD

Philippians 4:19
And this same God who takes care of me will supply all your needs from his glorious riches, which have been given to us in Christ Jesus.

TOILING

Aching head, filled with worries and stress
pounding, hounding with no recess
It throbs and it runs, it hurts, and it groans,
sometimes it seems it will never calm down.

Pain racks my back, it threatens to break
with each labored breath I take
yearning for rest, needing a place to lay
praying today will not be the day
my body gives way
to the pain that engulfs it as I toil.

Tired, weary eyes
threatening to close
though I stand all day
I struggle not to doze
lulled by the delicate pale light
shining through the doors
but I can't stop now
there's still much to do

so I continue working
toiling my way through.

Tired feet, dragging slowly here and there,
heavy-laden with tons of weights, barely getting anywhere.
They ache, and it seems, many miles they have run,
still they step, faltering but getting to the things that
need to be done.

Though daily laced with aches and myriad pains
this body works and works and works
striving for the gain
sit houses sweet memories of caring for my family
ensuring each child graduates college
It is fueled by big dreams for this family I adored
so every day I pick myself up knowing I'm stronger than the
day before.
Always believing, always hoping, always trusting
that things would work out just right
As I kept right on toiling
all through the day and night.

So today I look in the mirror, trying to see what's within,
hoping the good I do, and the love that I bring,
the strength, courage they will one day see,
and knowing as a mother, this is where I'm meant to be.

CONFESSION

Give me strength, Lord to do all that I have to do so I can take care of my family's needs. I admit that it's so hard and sometimes I feel like I can't go on. The physical pain is sometimes too much and on my own its difficult to get through each day. Please, Lord, give me the strength that I need to face today. I don't have to worry about tomorrow. Thank you for keeping me and for hearing my prayer. In Jesus' name. Amen.

THE WORD

Jeremiah 31:25
For I have given rest to the weary and joy to the sorrowing."
"I will refresh the weary and satisfy the faint

PENNILESS

Hunger like no other feeling
I've experienced before
a deep-seated emotion
a permanent resident
in my belly
in my soul
in my heart.

Hunger,
the stench of which
comes up to my nostrils

my stomach
my head
my heart.

Hopelessness
unlike anything I've seen before
permeates
my home
my yard
my space
my heart.

Daily I lay
in the squalor
of despair
heading nowhere
seeing no light
having no hope
knowing this is it
this is life
this is destiny.

PRAYER

Heavenly Father I ask You in the name of Jesus to remember me with the favor You have toward Your people. Heavenly Father I ask You in the name of Jesus to bless my hard work and help me prosper since it is written that 'the soul of the diligent shall be made rich.' (Proverbs 19:4) Bless the works of hands and help me to walk in the blessings you have stored up for me. In Jesus name, Amen.

THE WORD

Psalm 140:12
*But I know the Lord will help those they persecute;
he will give justice to the poor.*

WEIGHT-GAIN

I've struggled all my life
to be like the slim girl next door
and now that I'm an adult
I'm struggling even more
to like who I am
and not feel lesser than… anyone.

I want to be a woman
who's comfortable in her own skin
who oozes self confidence
flowing from deep within
but I am not she
she's far from who I am
I hate who I've become
I hate that I hate me
I feel less than … a complete woman.

I cry day and night
and get no respite
for the mirror doesn't lie
and no matter how I try
I just can't love the me I've turned out to be.

I've tried dieting
sometimes not eating at all
not caring I was hurting me
or that one day I may starve
still,
my waist bulges
my belly sags
my hips protrudes
my heart is sad.

Persons try to tell me
to stop hurting this body of mine
they don't understand
the need to feel sublime
for
I know I will be happy
when I become thin
I will be more confident in my new skin
Shopping will no more be a horror
Eating not such a daily struggle.
I will turn my life around
turn the world upside down,

life won't be so grim
because then I would be thin.

CONFESSION

Heavenly Father, I know You love me as I am. You said in Your Word that You love me with an everlasting love. That I am fearfully and wonderfully made.

I often criticize myself, compare myself to others, hate myself; please forgive me. I hate what I see in the mirror, I have bad thoughts about myself. I feel resentful, inferior and unworthy of your love which makes me unable to love You and others as I should.

Please help me love myself as I am, to see myself as You see me. Please help me to accept my body with all its beauty and imperfections just the way You made it. Teach me how to love me unconditionally....without limitations, boundaries or negativity. Help me to understand that I am beautiful as I am.

THE WORD

1 Samuel 16:7

But the LORD said to Samuel, "Do not look at his appearance or at his physical stature, because I have [refused him. For the LORD does not see as man sees; for man looks at the outward appearance, but the LORD looks at the heart."

WEIGHT-LOSS

I looked in the mirror and I feel really, really, grim
I'm fighting a battle and I'm struggling to win.
I keep losing weight and no one can tell me why
I feel totally depressed, wondering if I'm about to die.

The doctors don't know what's happening to me
except something's not quite right and it's there for all to see
I do all the test and the results conclude the same thing
All seems fine, nothing wrong within.

I'm going crazy, I'm losing my mind
people try hard to lose weight all the time
but this is different, something is terribly wrong
today I feel weak when a month ago I was strong
and no amount of rhetoric can put my mind at ease
I really need some answers, I need a full release.

I try to be positive, suppressing negativity
but it's difficult to be hopeful with a sick body
I worry that it's cancer and I'm staring death in the face
I feel my life is shortened and I'm about to prematurely end the race.
I can't sleep at night because I'm thinking all the time
as my fears keep playing over and over in my mind.

Oh I wish there was someone special on whom I could lean
to rock me when I'm scared and encourage me when I'm

weak
to dry the tears as they fall to the ground
to keep assuring me I'll always be around

No one wants to die while they're all alone
everyone needs someone to help them be strong
to help them share the uncertainty of life
to help them navigate in the darkest night.

so now I'm really, really scared
I have these feelings that are really, really weird
am I going to die?

CONFESSION

Lord, nothing is impossible with You. Nothing is too difficult for You. Nothing can hinder You. You can heal every kind of sickness, disease, infirmity, and pain. And You have promised to be my Healer. Therefore, I ask that right now, You cause Your healing power to flow mightily throughout every part of my body, throughout every fibre of my being, so that my health and healing will spring forth speedily at a supernatural rate. Heal my body and heal my mind. In Jesus name, amen.

THE WORD

Psalm 6:2

Have compassion on me, LORD, for I am weak.
Heal me, LORD, for my bones are in agony.

ILLNESS

We had a marvelous plan
when you agreed to be my husband
and it was all a thrill until the day I fell ill
now I seem only a shell of who I used to be
I am nothing like the woman
you enthusiastically married the one you carried
across the threshold.

I look in the mirror
and I'm tempted to ask
'who is she, staring at me?
in that body
skinny and weak?
This person who was rarely ever ill,
With boundless energy never content being still
this is not me...not me at all.

I seem to have disappeared
right before my face,
And now a gaunt sick stranger
stands in my place.
I live in a body I no longer know,
As the pains from this illness grow and grows and grow,
causing havoc in my life
diminishing all that once was
that once seemed so bright

but now every part of me aches
as my body trembles and shakes.

But you have been brave
never seeming to cave
under the pressure.
You stayed strong in caringnever ever complaining
that illness has intervened
in our picture-perfect scenethat started off so right
with butterflies and rainbows and beautiful light
in its place is an enduring love
inspired from heaven above
It will take us through
the darkness of the night.
I will always love you
until my dying breath
nothing can separate us two
not even the beckoning of death.

CONFESSION

Lord Jesus, thank you that you love me. I ask, in the name of Jesus, that you would heal this disease, that you would have compassion and bring healing from all sickness. In the Bible, I have read of miraculous healing and I believe that you still heal the same way today. I believe that there is no illness you cannot heal; after all the Bible tells of You raising people from the dead, so I ask for Your healing in this situation. If there are doctors or treatments that you would want to use to heal this disease, I pray that You would guide. I ask for wisdom and discernment about which treatments to pursue. In Jesus name, amen.

THE WORD

Exodus 15:26
...I will put none of the diseases upon thee, which I have put upon the Egyptians: for I am the LORD that health thee.

Section 2

Loosed

God cares about people. He is still healing. He's still fixing. He's still losing. He still ministers His grace and power to those who suffer from the oppressions of the devil. In His love and care He has provided healing and deliverance for all His children. Therefore,

Our weaknesses do not speak failure
our past does not speak defeat
our brokenness does not speak destiny eroded
our circumstances and situations do not define who we are.
Woman, you are loosed…it's time to LIVE.

Philippians 3:13
No, dear brothers and sisters, I have not achieved it,
but I focus on this one thing: Forgetting the past and looking
forward to what lies ahead, I press on to reach the end
of the race and receive the heavenly prize for which
God, through Christ Jesus, is calling us.

LOOSE

It was a simple word
flowing from the heart
a simple word giving
me a new start.
The crowd was there
but I didn't care
I needed Jesus more than I needed air
but how could I get to Him
through this crowd so incredibly thick
without and within.

I saw Him, He was reading from the scroll
He saw me, He looked deep within my soul.
He knew my spiritual infirmity
saw my chronic disability
I needed Him
and He knew, somehow He knew
the pain and torment that had me suffering
day after day
night after night.

Then He spoke
with full authority
The Words
the words that would set me free
the words that were music to my ears

the words I had never, ever heard
the words that would change my life forever
and bring a total makeover.

"Woman thou art loose"
loose, loose
Hallelujah! loose! Loose!
from illness and pain
wrinkles and stain
from by besetting infirmity
loose
for all eternity
........loose.

Hallelujah

I am loosed. I am no longer bound. I am no longer under the yoke of sin. Thank You God. Thank You that I am victorious through Christ Jesus, who is my strength, my fortress and my strong tower. In Jesus Name, Amen.

DECLARE IT!!!

I declare that I have been set free from sin and I am totally surrendered to God. My fruit will be to holiness, and the end, everlasting life. According to Romans 6:22, which says I am now free from the power of sin and have become a slave of God, now I do those things that lead to holiness and result in eternal life. In Jesus name, Amen.

Chapter 15

No Greater Love

To give one's life for someone else is the ultimate proof of love. God loves you no matter what trauma you may have gone through. During the night that Jesus was betrayed, He told His disciples of His divine destiny, His intention to give His life in exchange for mankind. He said "Greater love has no one than this, than to lay down one's life for his friends" (John 15:13). And then He set the ultimate example of love by going to the cross.

This kind of love is far deeper and more secure than any other love we will ever experience. It's this kind of love that binds the broken hearts, dries all tears from our eyes, is kind and compassionate towards us and empathizes with our infirmities.

There is no greater love than to lay down one's life…

WRONG ADDRESS

Spiritually we find ourselves residing at places
we are not meant to be
still we set down roots
staying there permanently.
Sometimes it's hard to get away
life seems to be passing us by everyday
before we know it
we are stuck
in a rut
or moving from place to place.

Worry Street is an easy place to stop
constantly fretting our daily lot.
making a big deal out of everything
finding no rest or peace within
being restive rather than resting
learning nothing of totally trusting…Him.

Soon Worry Street can become dilapidated
and must be torn down
making it easy to move all the way to the next town
residing on the street called Doubt
never certain of what life is about
trusting nothing and no one
thinking…I'm the only one who can….
care for me.

Then one-night Doubt street fell flat to the ground
so we packed and moved around
we found Despair Avenue and there we lay
hoping it was 'only' a temporary stay
Cause nothing about her inspired permanence
not the road, not the house, not the broken fence
life there was in a delicately poise between the eerie silence
and the overpowering noise

And just when life began to settle
we moved to a town called 'Little'
on Frustration road we found a room
filled to the brim with gloom and doom
no sun ever shone here
the days were laced with darkness and fear.
we knew another move was imminent
so we started scouting somewhere else to rent.

So now we're stuck in Desperation Village
with others like us just daily chilling
nothing ever changes here
and life is stained with fright and fear
so I think this is where we'll stay
since no one will drive us away
misery likes company you see
so we may even live for free.

But wait, these addresses are completely wrong
none of them are where we belong.
for you see
we're created to live on eternity street
daily enjoying joy and peace
living life full and free
protected from that one who comes to kill and steal.
God will be our landlord
as we all live in one accord
we can call on Him for all we need
for He's our provider, our Father indeed
He will keep us at rest
our pillow will be His chest.

HALLELUJAH,

I've been rescued from darkness to the marvelous light of Jesus. Thank You for your amazing power and work in my life. Thank You for rescuing me. Thank You for reconciling me to You. I was hopeless, wandering aimlessly, without stability, hope and peace; but Your incredible sacrifice allows me to have freedom and life in You. You are worthy! Amen.

DECLARE IT!!!

Your Word declares according to Ezekiel 34:12 that You will be like a shepherd looking for his scattered flock. ..You will find Your sheep and rescue them from all the places where they were scattered on that dark and cloudy day. …..I am stable, an heir to the covenant of promise, having a hope according to Your word in Ephesians 2:12

HE WANTS ME

I'm
frayed, worn
beaten, torn
troubled
wounded
hurt
used
abused
crushed
but still…. he wants me

I don't get it
I don't understand
I've been
victimized
ostracized
criticized
delegitimized, tagged and locked in a box
labelled 'no good'
but yet…He desires me

How could He still want…me?
He knows about

my
luggage
baggage
insecurities
inadequacies
trauma
fears
tears
He knows it all...

Yet....
He wants me
imperfect me
tainted, soiled...me.
So
He sought me
searched through the
rubble
garbage
anger
defenses
He had to have me.

Then I surrendered...
slowly
hesitantly....
Now,
He has me

and the miraculous happened
I can stand erect
no longer permanently bent
head downcast to the floor
…but now
I'm a daughter of The King
owning everything
with Him.

HALLELUJAH,

Your power is limitless, and Your forgiveness is endless. I know and believe that there's no pit so deep that your love can't reach, for as high as the heaven is from the earth so is Your love for me. Thank You Lord for chasing and pursuing me. May I live worthy of such incredible expression of love in Jesus' name, Amen.

DECLARE IT!!!

Lord Your word declares according to St. John 3:16 that You love me so much that You gave up Your only Son so that I shall not perish but have eternal life. You love me so much that You left ninety-nine other sheep to search for me. I am loved and cherished by You. I am valuable to You.

GOD CHOSE ME LONG BEFORE

I am no accident
God chose me
He reached down His hands
and refused to let me be
I was set free
from the dregs of sin

Long before I was conceived
God, You had for me a great plan
so I was intricately crafted
By Your Masterful hand.

Come, My God whispered to me,
follow me and fulfill
your destiny
There's so much for you to gain If you will trust
and call upon My Name.
I have a plan for you
from the very first day A plan that will never ever
go away
love, hope, and faith I will give to you.
prosperity, healing if you only knew
I'll carry you if I need to
and hold you when you pray.

I'll stand close by you
each and every day.
One day you will see
what I've been telling you.
the love that I've been saving
from the moment I created You.

HALLELUJAH,

I am no accident. I am no mistake. I am not an afterthought. God designed me long before I was born. I was created in His likeness and image. He created me with talents, gifts and unique abilities. You created me with creative mind, creative thinking and You have given me everything I need to succeed. In Jesus Name.

DECLARE IT!!!

Today I boldly declare that I am no accident and no mistake! God knew me before the earth was created; He called me before I was formed in my mother's womb.! God has a plan for me! I am purposeful. I declare this by faith in Jesus' name!

CHOSEN

He wanted me
and no one else would do,
He wanted me
and there was no settling
He had to have me
I was chosen.

I've always known He wanted me
He was relentless in His pursuit
Hunting me
as a hunter stalks his prey
I was to be His at all cost
nothing was to prevent His
ultimate take-over
He would have me
mind
body
soul.

How could I resist
such persistent wooing
such public display
of love
sacrifice
the ultimate price
death for me.

Me,
who would have none of Him
as I reveled in sin
thank God He never gave up
on me
Finally,
I'm His.

HALLELUJAH,

Lord, I am so glad that You knew me and called me even before I was conceived in my mother's womb. According to Your Word, I am no mistake, You have chosen me. Thank You Lord for choosing me. You have an awesome plan for my life. I ask You to help me uncover Your plan so I can get started on the road of obedience toward the fulfillment of what You brought me into this world to do! I pray this in Jesus' name!

DECLARE IT!!!

You declare in John 15:16 that I did not choose You, You chose me..." Therefore, I boldly declare that I am no accident, I am no mistake! You knew me before the earth was created; You called me before I was formed in my mother's womb. I am important to You.

MASTERPIECE

I am His masterpiece,
I'm one of a kind
God crafted and molded me
my heart, my soul, my mind.

I'm His masterpiece,
He fashioned and created every unique part
stamping purpose on me
right from the very start.

I'm His masterpiece,
God designed all of me
He has a purpose and plan
for all the world to see.

I'm His masterpiece
His crowning achievement
laden with gifts and talents
to fulfill my divine appointment.

I'm His masterpiece,
marvelous in every way
filled with divine empowerment
to live each and every day.

I am His masterpiece,
a stunning success
the image of His only Son
God's handiwork at its best.

I'm His masterpiece
His priceless work of art
full of divine potential
victory is mine at last!

HALLELUJAH,

I am God's masterpiece. I am fearfully and wonderfully made. I am created in His likeness and image. There is nothing substandard or inferior about me.

DECLARE IT!!!

I declare according to Ecclesiastes 3:11 that God has made everything beautiful for its own time....I am God's masterpiece.

INSCRIBED IN HIS HANDS

The Holy Spirit spoke to me today
and this is what He had to say
My precious child
nothing about you is hidden from me
everything in your life I see
I know exactly who you are

and I accept you warts and all.
I know your ways
I know your days
You're the most important of my
creation
see, I've inscribed you in the Palm of My hand.

My child,
this inscription
is permanent
it
cannot be
lost
annulled
blotted out
canceled
effaced
erased
removed
or
washed away.

It's legible
indelible
unforgettable
lasting
ingraining
unfading
here to stay.

LOOSE TO LIVE

The cross proved it
the nails could not remove it
the blood that flowed cemented it
my resurrection demonstrated it
my ascension secured it.

You my child
are valuable
irreplaceable
inestimable
costly
worth more than precious gold
priceless
you mean the world to Me
and that's how it will always be.

I was moved beyond tears
shocked at the words in my ears
I felt
adored
loved
cherished

beautiful
treasured
prized

revered
nourished
nurtured
p
held in high esteem

Now I know
now I understand
what it means to
be inscribed in my
Savior's hands.

HALLELUJAH

I am inscribed in my Savior's hand and nothing can ever erase the inscription. Praise God! I am His beloved daughter. I am His Heir. I will not let any voice, including my own, diminish or dismiss this truth. In Jesus name, Amen.

DECLARE IT!!!

According to I am inscribed in the Palm of God's hand. I matter to Him. My ways are directed by Him. I believe it, I receive it, I accept it…Lord please help me to live it. Amen

APPLE OF HIS EYES

The world has depersonalized me
a number assigned to me
an identification
stripped of all that makes me
unique
special
one of a kind.
But
not Him.

I am His
valued creation
His offspring
created in His image
His Royal Priesthood
chosen
precious
His finest
His choicest
His delight
cherished above all others
His daughter
I belong to Him.

Love unmatched
without borders

> without limits
> without conditions
> clean
> forgiven
> righteous
>
> The center of His plan
> the apple of His eyes.

HALLELUJAH

Lord God, I thank You that I am the apple of Your eyes. You love me, without limits, without borders, without conditions. The love You have for me is matched by no other love that the world has ever seen or ever will see! Remind me daily that You only want the best for me. Continue to shower me with Your blessings every second of every day that I live.

DECLARE IT!!!

I declare that I am the Apple of God's eyes. He Loves me. He favours me. His plans and purpose for me are perfect. I'm Hidden me in the shadow of Your wings according to.

.

FAVOURED

Lavishly, he pours His love on us
unhindered
unchecked
like a well-watered garden
a spring in a hot humid desert.

His favour surrounds us daily
through the opening and closing of doors
miracles
healings
provisions
protections
acceptance
happiness
success
unprecedented blessings
unexplained happenings
in our lives.

God favours women who are
obedient to Him
those who
give sacrificially
love Him wholeheartedly
submit to His will
renounces the world

take up the cross
and
follow Him.

HALLELUJAH

I am favoured by God. I put my trust in You. Thank You that Your favour, is upon me. Because of Your favour everything I do will succeed. Thank You, Lord, for the grace and glory that You give to me. You have withheld nothing good from me as I live a life that is pleasing to You. Everything good and perfect in my life comes from You, Lord. You, who are full of wisdom and grace, and never changing. I praise You in all I do. James 1:7

DECLARE IT!!!

I declare that God's favour encompasses me. Everywhere I go, everything I do, I am favoured by Him. I walk in His favour daily.

Chapter 16

Wanting Something New

Are you tired of being tired? Do you want something new? Do you want God to do a new thing in your life? Do you think your present circumstances make it impossible for you to achieve your destiny?

Take courage, be bold, the Word of God declares that God has made a way, carved a path, positioned you, refreshed you and is ready to launch you into your divine destiny. He wants you to come up and out of the ordinary and rise above your limits. So much is on the horizon, so much lies ahead, so much is waiting. There will certainly be bumps in the road, distractions and curves along the way, detours on the path but put your faith in God and speak NEW things into wilderness or desert seasons.

The old life has gone, a new life has begun!"
Receive it! Believe it! Embrace It! Live it!

WHO I'M CREATED TO BE

I've felt guilt and shame for many, many years,
living a life filled with fears
but I felt the love of God today,
and it took the darkness away
it happened so suddenly
my burden was lifted instantly.

I cried out to Him and He took my sin,
I opened the door and let Him in
now I wear a genuine smile,
one I haven't worn in quite a while.

Now I know it's going to be alright
no longer will I cry myself to sleep at nights
no more will I live in constant fear,
feeling that failure is always near.

I've given to Him my everything
releasing all the hurt within
all the anger in my heart I'd stored
thrown in a flash right out the door
I'm now ready to live the abundant life
given to me by Jesus Christ
The Lord and Master of my life.

His love so warm
so pure and true,
I could not believe my life
He could renew
He cleansed my soul
from the inside outIt was then and only then
I knew what love was about.

HALLELUJAH,

I know that you have a plan for my life. I know it's a good plan. I embrace your purpose. Enlarge my vision of You and enable me to trust in You through all the circumstances of my life, knowing that Your thoughts towards me are only good continually. In Jesus name, AMEN.

DECLARE IT!!!

God has a plan for me. It's a great plan, a comprehensive plan, a wholistic plan. A Plan to prosper me, protect me and preserve me. A plan to give me a great future and a lively hope. I boldly accept God's plan and purpose for my life. In Jesus name, Amen.

WANTING SOMETHING NEW

I've lived under the illusion of freedom
cocooned in the idea that freedom lies in the abundance
of things I possess.
Living the life of a pursuant
daily chasing
money
comfort
power
pleasure
security
acclaimnever understanding that the need to havethe need
to own
the need to possess
creates an endless cycle of pursuing
craving
chasing
always wanting to have........more

Today I ponder the chase
realizing that wanting more has no destination
no end in sight
it's like chasing a mirage
an endless pursuit leading nowhere
yet creating a never-ending cycle of owning and possessing
never satisfying
never stopping

never accepting
that this is it
I have enough.

Today I realize that this unquenchable desire for more
has brought me nothing but
heartbreak
loneliness
emptiness
insecurity
hollowness
a meaningless life hinging on nothing.

As I seriously contemplate the folly
of amassing
there's an unsettled feeling in my belly
in my heart
in my soul
a deep emptiness inside
creating a desire for something new
a new path
a new lease on life
a new relationship with someone other
than the things I possess

Today I desire peace
calm
a refreshing of my soul

comfort
relationship
friendship
Jesus
the Christ
eternity

HALLELUJAH

The new has come. I praise You Lord for this newness of life that comes from knowing You. Continue to fill my heart completely with Your love and presence. May you help me to walk confidently in this new life allowing nothing to derail my walk with You. In Jesus name, Amen.

DECLARE IT!!!

Today I declare according to 2 Corinthians 5:17, my old habits, desires, needs, attitudes have gone and have been replaced by a new outlook. I embrace this change in me and welcome with excitement and anticipation the newness that will be unfolded in my walk with Christ.

SEARCHING

Prowling about
like a hungry lion
digging and searching for every
piece of the puzzle tocomplete me.
Pursuing always the illusion
of total freedom
always pursuing

money

comfort

power

pleasure

wealth

acclaim

with no eternal aim.

But it has been an endless road of pursuing more
and more and more
with no goal in sight
a never-ending road
that had no destination

no stop

no end

just the chasing of a mirage
ending in heartbreak
I wasn't enjoying the journey
I wanted something new

Fresh
I wanted God
so I went looking for Him
seeking him high and low
looking for him in nature, in church, in other people.
Not realizing I don't need to go anywhere or look beyond myself to find him.
He had been waiting for me the whole time.
So, I surrendered and allow myself to be found
by Him.

HALLELUJAH

I don't have to search anymore. Abba Father let me see you. Draw me closer to You so that I can see Your face in a way I never have before. Remind me that You live in my heart. Help me to trust Your love for me. In Jesus' Name. Amen.

DECLARE IT!!!

I declare Hebrews 11:6 that as I come to You; You are and will continue to reward me for sincerely seeking You.

WHISPERS OF THE LORD

I am important to God who knows my name
who sees everything about me,
and loves me just the same.
Daily He whispers
sweet things in my ears
erasing all the shame
that has bombarded me through the years.

There is nothing beyond your reach, He says
you're my treasure, for you I bled
you're my creation,
and though sometimes you drift
you're and will always be
my very , very precious gift.

You're my workmanship
handcrafted
fashioned
purposed
to do
good
beautiful
and
powerful things.

You're talented,
creative beyond measure

> brilliant, gorgeous,
> talented, fabulous.
> You are not small
> You are a child of mine
> You are meant to shine
> Created to manifest the glory of God.

HALLELUJAH

God loves me so much that even when I was a sinner, He sent His Son, Jesus Christ, to die for me. The blood of Jesus cleanses me and makes me free. Sin no longer has dominion over me. God loves me in the midst of my imperfections and weakness. Therefore, I appreciate and cherish who I am in Him. I love myself, fully, totally, unconditionally. I am God's child. I am precious. I am forgiven, cleansed, restored, healed and clothed in His beauty! I am amazing! Thank you, Lord, in Jesus name, Amen.

DECLARE IT!!!

I declare that I AM God's workmanship, created in Christ unto good works according to Ephesians 2:10.

GETTING PASSED THE PAST

The unknown beckons
me to come
I really want to go
But the pain of the past to continues to invade the present
making my progress slow
holding hostage my future
but I'm so afraid of moving forward
I'm stuck in the past right now.

I know yesterday is gone
and should stay where it belongs
I know I need to embrace the future
I'm in this place too long.

Tormented by memories
battered and blistered by the burden of brokenness
I want to say no to them
to close my heart from within
but they just won't release me
so, I continue daily to sink
in the abyss of regrets and pity
which dulls my ability to think.

It's ironic really
this place I am right now
cause nothing in my past

provided any fun.
There were so many hurts
and pains in my life
so why am I hanging on
afraid to leave them all behind.

I can't refuse anymore
I must say goodbye
I must release the negative
be joyful with the new life I've been given
I must live for today
and refuse to stay
where I once was.

Yes,
that past is the past for a reason.
It's been, and now it is gone,
there's no way to fix it.
It's time to bury it and move on.

HALLELUJAH,

I am a product of my past, but I'm not defined by it. It does not dominate me nor does it determine my outcome. Lord, You are doing a new thing and I thank You. You are opening new doors, new windows of opportunity, new thoughts and ideas, new interest and new attractions. Thank You, Lord.

DECLARE IT!!!

You declare according to Isaiah 43:19 that You are doing a new thing! Its springing up; You are making a way in the wilderness and streams in the wasteland for me. The past is behind me and a glorious future is before me. I open my hands and receive it now, In Jesus name, Amen.

LET IT GO

I've held on to the memories long enough
It's time to let them go
no longer can I just exist
merely swimming with the flow.

The past has been a rough
and tiresome season
now I must move on
despite the mountains of reasons
it wants to hang around
trying to disrupt this happiness I have found.

Many won't let me forget it
reminding me everyday
about the tons of mistakes I've made
my many failures along the way.

Now their focus has become
The person I used to be,

They see nothing of how far I've come.
nothing of this new me.

I cannot change what happened,
no matter how hard I try,
I can't change those I hurt,
no matter how many times I cry.

It takes more than courage to be released of yesterday
when you've been battered and hurt
bruised and scarred
and left like a dog in the dirt.

But today I'm letting go
today I'm moving on
I can no longer stay here
I must get ready to live my purpose
my destiny to wear.

HALLELUJAH,

I let go of the past, its traumas, hurts and torments. I hold on to Your instruction to throw all my anxieties and all my cares on You. I receive Your loving presence around me and within me. I trust You that when I am feeling overwhelmed, I will receive Your peace, love and courage. I let go of problems and challenges in order to receive Your guidance. I let go and trust You, I know that I will not fall for You will catch me if I slip or stumble. In Jesus' name, Amen.

DECLARE IT!!!

I declare that there is greatness within me. My success is already decided, and I stand in my victory. I will live in the present and I will focus on forgetting the past and looking forward to what lies ahead. Phil. 3:13 , In Jesus name, Amen.

NAKED BEFORE THE LORD

Vulnerable
readable
unhidden
unbridled
unencumbered
I stood before the Lord.

Nothing hidden
nothing covered
naked
bare
for His eyes to see.

Sharing everything
withholding nothing
all my secrets to him I tell
about my past
my mistakes
the road I was on to hell.

My deepest longings,
all my hurts and all my fears,
the things that make me sad
my fears and my tears.

It's so great knowing I can go to Him
morning, noon and night,
He never ever turns me away,
always give ear to my plight.

There's no one that comes close to Him in my life
He's my closest friend.
In Him I'll always confide.
I'm growing to love Him
more and more each day
and I can't imagine living without Him
since He has become my mainstay.

So today I place my hope in you Lord
the One who I adore
for me there's no other
that I could ever love more.

HALLELUJAH,

I thank You for this new freedom I've found in You. Lord, teach me how to choose only Your way today so each step will lead me closer to You. Help me walk by Your Word and not my feel-

ings. Teach me how to be honest with You at all times even when I don't totally understand what You are doing. Help me to keep my heart pure and undivided. Protect me from my own careless thoughts, words, and actions. And keep me from being distracted by the things I want, the things I desire. In Jesus name, Amen."

DECLARE IT!!!

I rest in the truth of Psalm 86:13, Great is your love toward me.'

Chapter 17

Becoming Me

Have you wondered whether you can actually move into the full purpose and destiny God has for you? Do you hunger for something bigger? Something greater? Do you want to break out of the self-defeating cycle of repeated patterns and habits? Do you want to be more than just a survivor? Do you want to be an overcomer? I have great news for you!!! God's intention is for you to become the 'you' you were created to be. You were not designed to be who others expect You to be. You were created to become all that God planned for You to be from the very beginning of time. He has more for You than just merely eking out an existence day after day. He has a great purpose for your life.

Now is the time to embrace the fullness of your purpose! Now is the time to live life on purpose and with purpose.

Psalm 57:2
*I cry out to God Most High,
to God who will fulfill His purpose for me.*

BECOMING...ME

A woman of substance and worth
I yearn to be,
filled with Your Holy Spirit
transforming every inch of me.

A woman who embraces truth, honesty, integrity
despite the situations I face,
standing always for righteousness
as one who has experienced grace.

A woman of purpose
trusting in Your plan,
knowing You have charted a path for me
guided by Your own hand

A woman of promise,
standing on Your word;
holding on to all the truths
I have experienced, seen and heard.

A woman of mercy and compassion
for each and everyone

who is trapped by sin
and under Satan's command.

A woman who will stand sure
and never compromise her faith
with the blings and the things
that in the shadows wait.

A woman who loves God
and place Him above all else
who lives a life of full surrender
and on His wisdom always depend.

A woman in whom
others will see
the light of Jesus always
radiating through me
knowing my destination is not just
here and now
but forever all through eternity.

HALLELUJAH,

God You have forgiven my sins and remember them no more. I am now clean within and I now live to please You. Lord help me to walk in my purpose. Father, I pray Psalm 27:11, show me Your way Lord and lead me on a level path. As I grow and evolve in You, I thank You for opening all the doors for me that only

You can open and closing the ones that You have not ordained to fulfill my purpose. In Jesus name!

DECLARE IT!!!

*I declare according to **Psalm 37:5, 23** that as I commit my ways to You Lord and trust in You, You will bring destiny to pass. I declare that my steps are established by the Lord and You take pleasure in my way. I thank You for taking pleasure in me and for establishing every step I take. In Jesus Name, Amen*

FROM RAGS TO RICHES

Entrenched in the gutter of sin
darkness stained my heart within
struggled to make ends meet
daily facing devastating defeat
I could find no peace inside
bombarded by satan's taunts and lies.

This was how I came to the Lord
beaten, crushed, torn.
I had nothing but a broken heart
battered and bruised
I needed a new start.

A new lease on life to me was given
all my sins were forgiven
I then began to see
who I was designed by God to be.'

I discovered I was now held
in the palm
of His hand
and for me He had a marvelous plan
which did not end at redemption
and is unfolding step by step.
Now I'm soaring to new heights with Him
daily unlocking the potential within
a well-watered garden I've become
with leaves shooting up to the sun.
The rags of sin have been torn way
and at the top I aim to stay
as I walk confidently in this authority
and blessed freedom He has given to me.

I now know I will
achieve it all
fearing not that I could fall,
embracing
prosperity and success
a life without pity and regrets
that was how it was destined to be
A life lived abundantly.

HALLELUJAH.

I am no longer living aimlessly. God has a plan for my life from the beginning of time. His plan is both good and per-

fect. Lord Jesus help me to believe and live Your plan, in Jesus name, Amen.

DECLARE IT!!!

Thank You God that you have a glorious plan for me. Plans to prosper me and not harm me, to give me a bright future and lively hope according to Jeremiah 29:11. I declare I am Your daughter and You take pleasure in my prosperity (Psalm 35:27).

CONNECTING WITH JESUS

Its incomprehensible
unfathomable
a mystery even
difficult to process
defies all logic
or reason
this connection with Jesus.

It's alarming
yet transforming
regenerating
refreshing
life changing
this connection with Jesus.

It fuels
my
body

my Heart
my Soul
my Mind
creating purpose in my life
this connection with Jesus.

Others
sense it
see it
feel it
want it
this connection with Jesus.

I can't lose it
I will seek to embrace it
cherish it
walk in it
live it daily
this connection with Jesus

HALLELUJAH,

Your love for me is not based on my performance. You love me warts and all. As the deer longs for streams of water (Psalm 42:2) help me to always yearn for You. Take me deeper in Your Word, in Your presence and in my prayer life. May I always bring pleasure to You. Give me joy in Your presence and help me to bring joy into the lives of others. In Jesus' name, amen.

DECLARE IT!!!

Your Word declares that If I remain in You and Your Words remain in me, I shall ask whatever I wish, and it will be done for me, John 15:7 Your Words cannot lie so I declare that everything promised to me according to Your will be given to me as I read and obey Your Words. In Jesus name, Amen.

HE TAKES MY MESS

I'm feeling disappointed today
parts of my life
just seem to be wasting away
like a puzzle with hundreds of tiny pieces
all mismatched and out of place
defeats here failures there
regrets everywhere
reality way too difficult to bear.

Parts of my life
hanging on tenterhooks
pieces missing, sections
failing
nothing thriving.
Nothing for me works
nothings for me stays
nothing to pull me
from beneath the dirt.

That's the life
I gave to the Lord
defeated
broken
torn

He took it! Hallelujah! my sad messed up life
He took it!
my mistakes, failures and strife
He took it!
my soul covered in sin
He took it!
and made me clean within
He took it! and the broken pieces he mends.
He took it all!
and made me His friend
so
I only need to take Him at His Word and on His promises depend.
and if to His words I stay true
there is no limit to what I can do.

HALLELUJAH,

I am happy that when I am weak Lord, You are strong. Remind me today that when I am tempted to give up or give in You will help me to keep going. Grant me a cheerful spirit when things don't go my way. And give me courage to do whatever needs to be done. That's amazing. But what's most amazing is that the Savior of the world would desire to take my mess and love me just the same. Amen.

DECLARE IT!!!

Your word declares that You take my mess. Hallelujah!! You are my help and my deliverer; you are my God. You will always fight for me, You will always protect me, You will always deliver me, according to Psalm 40:17. I will stand on Your Word. In Jesus name, Amen.

WOMAN…YOU ARE LOOSED

The devil had a hold on me
from the day I was born
he completely controlled me
he had my heart.
he willingly became my master
and at first it was great
he gave me everything to
make my life luxurious on earth.

Then it all went awry
he wanted every inch of my life
he wanted every piece of me
morning, noon and night.
My joy he slowly took away
while he stole from me in every way.
he took my peace

my joy
my stability
leaving me destitute and disheartened
my world completely darkened
fearing nothing good would ever happen.
I was alone, locked in a nightmare.
broken, discouraged and bare.

Then one day I chose a new Master
He opened my eyes, and
with Him I started over.
I saw reflected in His merciful face
the completeness of His forgiveness
the vastness of His grace.
He became my
greatest friend
on whom I can depend.

I know that He will lead me
daily as I trod.
So to Him I gave my life
every inch of Me
Holding nothing back
trusting Him completely
what a great privilege by Him to be used
now that I live a life of a woman who is loosed.

HALLELUJAH

Thank you, Lord for setting me free. Help me stand in that freedom and not be entangled again with a yoke of bondage. Lord God, you are my strength. Hold my hand in my weakness and teach me how to trust in Your power to keep me for with you, there's nothing to fear, nothing to worry about. In Jesus Name, Amen.

DECLARE IT!!!

I declare according to Galatians 5:1 that I have been set free by Jesus. I will stand firm by the power of God, and not be entangled again in the yoke of bondage. I have the power to do this because the Holy Spirit lives in me and will help me.

LOOSED TO LIVE....NOTHING ELSE MATTERS

Free at last, it is finished
life has triumphed over death
the power of sin has been broken
my mind has been reset.

I have been snatched from sin
Christ now lives within
my heart has a new flow
Christ lives and reigns forever more.

'Self' no longer has dominion
no longer shouts condemnation

God is my father
satan is no longer my master.

I now experience the abundant life
freed from all misery and strife
there's peace in my soul
Hallelujah, I'm whole.

Now I'm complete
thank you God, for setting me free
from the power of sin, you have rescued me
my soul is ready for eternity
I'm loosed and that's all that matters
You my creator is now my 'Abba' father.

HALLELUJAH,

I am loosed; I am no longer bound. Sin no longer has dominion over me. Satan's hold on my life is shattered by the blood of Jesus Christ. Thank You for the life I now have in Christ. I ask You to fill me with the Holy Spirit so that I can be guided by You and not carry out the desires of the flesh. I declare my total dependence and submission to You. I believe the truth of Your Word. In Jesus Name, Amen.

DECLARE IT!!!

I declare that Jesus loves me, rescues me, protects me, acknowledges my name.

He answers when I call on Him and He is with me in trouble. He will deliver me and honour me according to Psalm 91:14-15. I now walk in total freedom, without condemnation. Sin no longer has control over me.

LOOSED TO PRAISE

Dark days
dull days
gloomy days
once took my praise away.
my focus was split
I was a misfit
in the Kingdom.

Today, I got my praises on
Hallelujah, my load is gone
all that I am I give to You Lord
my heart, my soul, my mind, my body
all in one accord.

I praise and worship Your Name
in my heart Lord, live, rule and reign
inhabit my hands, head and feet.
live in me permanently

I raise my hands in absolute adoration…
as I lift you up in worship and exaltation!

I surrender to you my everything
I'm loosed to praise you, to dance and sing.

I'll make worshipping You Lord,
my daily lifestyle,
allowing it to inform everything I do
not just my singing of spiritual songsbut in my everyday happenings too

So no more will I let my situations win
no more will I mess with sin
You are and will always be the one for me!
Hallelujah I'm loosed for eternity!

HALLELUJAH,

My shackles are gone, the chains that held me so tightly have been broken. God, Your unfailing love shatters my mind. I cannot fathom it, I cannot express it adequately but I am grateful and with all my heart I will praise You. Thank You for loosing me so that I can Praise You. Thank You for setting me free from all that had me bound. I thank You today for the gift of praise. In the name of Jesus, I pray. Amen.

DECLARE IT!!!

I declare that 'with all my heart I will praise you, O Lord my God. I will give glory to Your name forever.' I will sing unto You LORD as long as I live: I will sing praise to You my God while I have my being according to Psalm 104:33. You are great and my lips will praise You! In Jesus Name, Amen.

LOOSED TO SUCCEED

Dear failure
I serve you notice today
success is here
and it is here to stay.
Today is the day
I stop believing your lies
that my circumstance will not change
even if I try.

So hear me failure
you just have to go
you have been my friend
and my status quo
but as cozy as you have been to me
you have interfered with my divine destiny.

So now that I'm loosed
and a 'shift' has taken place
there is no room for you
in my new space.
Success has taken over
he's large and in charge
he has totally transformed

this unbelieving heart.
he has a lot in store for me
and all he asked is that I simply believe.

HALLELUJAH,

Lord God, Your blessings abound in my life. Thank You that You have blessed me in every area of my life. Thank You for replacing failure, fear and despair with confidence, hope and courage. I now know that in You success is guaranteed. In Jesus name, Amen.

DECLARE IT!!!

According to 1 Chronicles 4:10, Lord You bless me and expand my territories, Your hand is with me, and You keep me from all trouble and pain!" Thank You God.

LOOSE TO WALK IN AUTHORITY

Hallelujah! I have been set free
by Jesus who now lives in me
I no longer belong to him
who had me bounded by sin.

No longer a slave
freedom He came and gave
Jesus is now the only One
for two masters I will not serve
for Him only my heart is reserved.

There's therefore now no condemnation
since I'm a new creation
sin therefore has no power
to enslave me to its torture.

I resist satan
his lies
his taunts
his disguise.

I have prayer as my shield
so to failures I will not yield
I don my armour everyday
keeping satan miles away.

While I live on this side of eternity
I take comfort in my authority
endowed to me by Jesus Christ
who is now Lord and Master of my life.

Challenges I know will come my way
but I also know they won't come to stay
so I will not entertain them in my life
I will stand in the authority of Jesus Christ
knowing I walk by faith, not by sight
Victorious I stand in my Lord's Power and Might.

HALLELUJAH,

I now walk in the authority of Jesus Christ, my creator, redeemer, Lord and King. I thank You for giving me authority to rule on earth. Teach me to exercise this authority in my life, my community, and my nation. In Jesus name, Amen.

DECLARE IT!!!

Lord You declare that You have given me authority over all the power of the enemy, to walk among snakes and scorpions, and crush them and nothing will injure me according to St. Luke 10:19. I accept this authority to live above my problems, issues and circumstances as I walk this new life in Jesus' name...Amen

Chapter 18

Freedom

It's the desire of every woman to live a life of freedom - to love, and hope, and dream; and to experience joy, and peace, and satisfaction. We all want to be free to enjoy the abundant, purposeful life that God has planned for us. God is calling us away from bondage, despair, depression, failure, superstition, error, bondage, deception, guilt, depravity, ignorance and anything else that's preventing us from living free in Christ Jesus. He is calling us to a life of liberty in Him.

So if the Son sets you free, you will be free indeed.

FREED

You saw me struggle
you saw me fall.
you saw me weak
when I really wanted to stand tall
you saw me give up
thinking I couldn't win
as I fought valiantly the demons trapped within.

You did nothing to help me
you laughed with glee
happy for the triumph
you finally had over me you expected me to die
as daily I cried and cried
you wanted me to continue believing
all your whispered lies.

You isolated me, told me no one cared
I believed you
and allowed you to fill
my heart with fear
I knew I had fallen and needed restoration
still I lived under your condemnation.
I became your slave, giving up my right
but you used it to terrorize me every day and night.
I never gave up even when you had me on my knees
I know you thought you had won
as you reveled in my desperate pleas.

You never thought I would rise
never thought I could ever be strong
but you were wrong
you never counted to whom I now belong.
You didn't think about the power
He would infuse into me How He would transform my life
energize my very being
you thought he would drive me away
turn away His holy face
you thought nothing of His Amazing grace.

Now I'm free
you no longer have dominion over me
I am truly free
enjoying life abundantly
I'm free
having peace within
no longer bound by shackles and chains of sin.
I'm free
living a life of prosperity
I'm free
walking in my divine authority
I am free
free to be
free

HALLELUJAH,

I am free. There are no more chains holding me Heavenly Father, thank You for doing the work so I may live free. May I no longer seek to earn Your approval but live a life from the truth that I am already free, loved, and Yours. I love You. Everything that is unlike You in my life is broken by the power of the Holy Spirit, in Jesus name, Amen.

DECLARE IT!!!

God You declare in Your Word that if the Son sets me free, I am free indeed. (John 8:36). I declare today that I have complete freedom in You, I am free from the pain of sin, the guilt and shame that wants to reside with me daily. I declare that You have equipped me with the power to walk in this freedom.

FREED FROM PRISON

For a long time I felt locked away
merely existing from day to day,
wearing daily my perfect *façade*
hoping no one discovers I'm flawed.
Living behind my prison wall
battered and bruised each time I fall
having no one on whom to call.
I felt sentenced to a prison cell
over time my mind began to shell, as I sank deeper and
deeper in my pit
with no hope of surviving it.

Then one day Grace found me
and promised me eternity,
Jesus opened my prison door
and miraculously set me free.
I began to see
that with certainty
I can be that woman of worth
living my purpose in my sojourn on earth.

I was gloriously free
freed from self-indulgence,
freed from self-obsession,
freed from self-pity,
freed from self-righteousness,
freed from the sin that was
reigning within.

There's a new joy in my heart
today
It's an assurance no one can take
away,
It's laden with
Happiness
Purpose
Contentment
Fulfilment
Freedom.

HALLELUJAH,

Thank you, Lord for setting me free. Help me stand in that freedom and not be get tied up again in slavery to the law – Gal. 5:1. Thank you, for the new life you have given me – saving me when I was dead in trespasses and sins. – Eph. 2:1. For the victory I have through Jesus Christ. – 1 Cor. 15:57. For Your truth which has set me free. – John 8:32 In Jesus mighty name, Amen.

DECLARE IT!!!

I declare Lord that you have set me free, therefore, I am free indeed according to John 8:36. Sin no longer has dominion over me. I am free to live the abundant life you have destined for me.

Chapter 19

New Beginnings

We have all experienced setbacks, disappointments, mistakes and failures throughout our lives. We sometimes allow these mistakes, setbacks, failures and disappointments to enslave us to the point that we never enjoy the full life that God has given to us. We never walk in our divine purpose and we never believed great things will work out for us. However, God encourages us to *forget the former things and not to dwell on the past. See, He says 'I am doing a new thing! Now it springs up; do you not perceive it?'* (Isaiah 43:18-19).

God wants to do a new thing in our lives. **Revelation 21:5** And He who sits on the throne said, "Behold, I am making all things new " *Do you* want a fresh start? A new beginning? *A brand-new lease on life?* What new thing do you want today? He is doing a new thing. A new thing is a good thing. He is bringing the dead things in our lives back to life! Let go of the past, live life to its fullest and embrace the new season.

THE INNER COURT

Flesh wants to stay in the Outer Court
unwilling to tap into
the supernatural realm,
missing out on experiencing
the glory and presence of God.
Not understanding that
His Spirit
no longer dwells in a building.

We fail to move closer
to God's ultimate purpose for our lives
we have yet to understand
that we are the church –
each one of us.
So we continue to fail to live
according to the pattern
He prepared for us
the instruction He provided us
the spiritual blueprint He created for us

Instead we are content to live on
the crust
the crumbs

practicing
a form of godliness
a resemblance of Holiness
but falling short of
the power thereof.

We seem not to understand that
when our relationship with God is sanctified
set apart,
protected
cemented
honoured
cherished
covered from within,
we are empowered to handle anything that comes from
without.

For with Him
we are
courageous
fearless
bold
confident
In
who He is
Who we are
Who we are in Him.

HALLELUJAH

Father, I praise You for the Inner Court experience. I thank you that You want to move me beyond the superficial and into a life where flesh is slain and You alone are glorified. I surrender my life to You. Help me to lay aside anything that blocks my relationship with You and wants to keep me in the Outer Courts. Speak to me. Guide me. I worship You. In Jesus' name. Amen

DECLARE IT!!!!

I declare today that You LORD are my strength and my song, and You have given me victory. I declare I am not fighting for victory; I am fighting from a place of vic- tory according to Exodus 15:2 which says The Lord is my strength and my song; he has given me victory.

A NEW DAY

Today,
I topple the idols in my life
I start walking a new path
never looking back
not allowing the old self
to make a comeback

Today,
I declare fear slain
buried underground to remain
It has interfered for far too long
making me weak where

I once was strong.
Refusing to give my dreams a try
blindly believing the enemy's lies.

Today
I take back my life
renounce negative words
and soul ties
finding strength where once I was weak
leaving the shallow, wading in the deep
Realizing who is standing at the end
My Master, my Father, my Friend.

Today
life starts afresh
my Master's DNA is in my flesh
I will win, I shall conquer, if I but try
I can fly, I can soar, I can touch the sky
I only need to believe
my dreams are possible
if they are conceived.
I need only to trust in my Savior's promises
as I live my new realities.
Today.......

HALLELUJAH

.... it's a brand new day in my life. Lord I thank You for the strength You provide. I thank You for equipping me with the

ability to conquer all my fears. God, please steer me in the right direction and show me the path I need to take. Help me daily to realize that all my dreams are possible, that success and prosperity are a part of Your plan for my life. Most of all God, help me to build my faith and pursue all the ideas and goals you have planted in me. In Jesus' name…Amen

DECLARE IT!!!

I declare that God is doing something new in my life. New beginnings are unfolding, fresh new creative ideas are being birthed within me, new doors are opening to me, new opportunities are coming my way, in Jesus name, Amen.

…ONLY GOD

Only God can
take a life
flawed, bruised
broken,
laden with
sin and guilt
and
transform it
reform it
recreate it
reposition it.

only God can
take a life
trapped
lacking purpose
lacking direction
and
Energize it
Increase it
Give it meaning.

Only God can
take a life of stress and
deep sadness
a life repressed
oppressed
daily pressed
and
give it
calm
peace
purpose
power,

Only God
our Creator
Father
Redeemer
Savior
Now friend

Only God
fixes the unfixable
loves the unlovable
stabilizes the unstable

Only God
favours the helpless
created miracles from my mess
shoulders my burden
relieves my stress.
Nobody but God
who placed the stars in the sky
dried every tear I ever cried.

God's
love
is
unconditional
extraordinary
vast
pure
dependent
on no one
but You, God.

HALLELUJAH,

Lord, you are faithful in all things. Your promises endure forever, and there is no limit to Your miracles. In Your hands all things are possible. You are the one who conquered death and made a place for us in heaven. May I never cease to sing Your praises. In your name I pray, Amen.

DECLARE IT!!!

We decree and declare that ALL THINGS ARE POSSIBLE WITH GOD according to Luke 18:27 which says, "What is impossible for people is possible with God. When God speaks all of creation stops and obeys! **Nothing is impossible***! Nothing! You, God are* **more than enough***.*

BEYOND OUR LIMITATIONS

I refuse to stay in this static place anymore
I must move beyond the door
of despair
desperation
frustration
fear
doom and
gloom.

I see
the glorious future set for me
from the beginning of time.

I move beyond the limits
placed upon my life,
and move into the plans
revealed through Jesus Christ.

I move forward
one step at a time
knowing God has gone ahead
to pave this way of mine.

By faith I take tiny steps,
towards those goals
I gained the courage to set
I remain confident and persistent
knowing victory is ahead
if I daily listen to the heavenly voice
Whispering inside my head.

You have given me the power to overcome
to be focused on the things
I set out to do
knowing no matter how hard it gets for me
I have the will to press through
never giving up
when things get tough
but trusting that if I fail
God will pick me up.

You sustain me when I
mess up
You make me strong daily
refilling my cup
You tell me there is nothing
I can't do
I am powerful and strong
victorious in you!

HALLELUJAH,

Lord, I thank you for freeing me, freeing me from the chains that bound me. Lord through You I can experience abundant life, I can live life without limits, live life on purpose. You have set me free, I now have a new outlook on life. I am thankful for Your gift of salvation, for eternal life. I am grateful for the inheritance You have given me. I am thankful that I can talk with You and can experience the beauty of Your Presence.

DECLARE IT!!!

Lord, You declare according to John 10:10 that You have come that I will have a rich and satisfying life, and have it to the full. I declare it is not too late to accomplish everything You God have purposed for me since the beginning of time. I have not missed my window of opportunity. I declare that I am creative, innovative, driven, focused and intentional.

DREAMING AGAIN

I stopped dreaming many years ago
My life was a mess
Totally out of control
So I packed all my dreams
In my wooden chest
Placed it under my bed
For eternal rest.
Nothing would come of them
Nothing good I thought
No prosperity, no success
They'd all come to naught.
No one would know of them
To no-one I would confess.
They were dead to me
So under my bed I let them be.

Then one day I gave my heart to Christ
Making Him the Lord of my life
I experienced His amazing grace
Transforming my life and my space.
It soon became clear to me
I was created to live purposefully
God has a plan formulated perfectly
it has my name engraved, etched indelibly
A plan for a hope, a future, prosperity

LOOSE TO LIVE

A plan made just for me,
stamped "Victory".

Then one day I felt it
a gentle tug, a stirring in my soul
a bidding by my Master
to make me
totally whole
a calling to come unto Him
shelter from the rain
and just like that, I started dreaming again.

I then realized my dreams were not new
but the same ones i had hidden when i hadn't a clue
now they seem just glorious
getting bigger in my head
without an ounce of fear, not a single shred of dread
and with renewed vim and vigor
my dreams beckoned to be fed
i fed them hope
expectancy
determination
perseverance
I now knew I would succeed
for God was now my Master
the holder of my dreams
and now I know success was already guaranteed.

HALLELUJAH,

Thank You that though I wasted many years You have helped me to start dreaming again. Thank You for reviving those dead dreams and bringing them back to life. Thank You for giving me the courage to take the first step. Thank You for being there for me when I fall or make a mistake in chasing our God-sized dream. Thank you for Your promise to cheer me on and encouraging me to try again. Thank you that I do not have to walk this journey alone Heavenly Father.

DECLARE IT!!!

Lord Your Word in Proverbs 21:5 tells me that good planning and hard work lead to prosperity. I decree and declare that my dreams will bring me success in all areas of my life. My plans will lead me to abundance in all areas of my life. I wake up with purpose, direction, and meaning every day of my life.

MAKEOVER

Who I was, I no longer am
the life I now live is greater than
all I had
It goes far beyond
the outer man
clothes
shoes money
hair

nails
house
cars
clubs
stars
satisfying self
waking up with loads of regrets.

So I've left that life behind
given Jesus my broken, tired life
not sure what he would make of it
but knowing it was a better fit.

Nothing prepared me for what he would do
recreating me from head to shoe
placing me under His spiritual cover
giving me a divine makeover.

He started at my head
stabilizing my mind
transforming my thoughts
making them divine.

Then it was time to transform my heart
that was a real work of art
for it was buried beneath loads of filth and dirt,
pain and hurts
anger and hate

resigned to its fate.
My mind he had to recreate
to produce a clean slate
He had to work to make it clean
gave His blood to make it pristine.

My sins did not deter Him at all
He chiseled and chiseled away the dross
It was challenging at first
toppling idols were the worst
but they had to go
there was no other way
Christ is now my Master and He's here to stay

My lips he had to cure
from gossiping, lying and much more
they needed to be put under control
so integrity could be restored
submitting my tongue was the only way
or the consequences I would continue to pay
so I quickly gave it to Him
and allowed Him to cleanse me from within.

Then it was time to cleanse my feet
to ensure they were ready to trample defeat
as I trod the by ways day by day
encouraging others to come my way
He made them sturdy, fit and strong

LOOSE TO LIVE

to withstand the pressure as I travel along
not buckling at a slight or strong whim
but standing straight and tall with vigor and vim.

The makeover seemed almost complete
and I was ready to sit at my Lord's feet
but He had something else up His sleeve
to make me fit for eternity.

My circle He had to clean
some friendships I had to wean
it was really hard to say goodbye
to some who were my ride and die
but I knew it was a must
so I let them go with little fuss
ensuring nothing soiled my soul
for eternity with Jesus was my number one goal.

Faith He knew I would really need
to be protected from satan's schemes
so my tank he filled up
and overflowed my upturned cup
I was now fit and ready to go
filled with confidence and the brightest glow
ready to face him who came to kill and steal.
though his strength is limited, it's very real
but my victory in Jesus is already sealed.

HALLELUJAH,

Lord You are doing a new thing in my life. I want to be a lover of God and thirst after You daily (Psalm 42:1-2a). Teach me how to align my heart with Yours. I recommit myself as a woman after Your heart. I choose to seek Your face (Psalm 27:8). In difficult times, open my heart to receive Your revelation. Hide me in Your sanctuary , place me out of reach on a high rock (Psalm 27:5).

DECLARE IT!!!

Lord You declare according to 2 Corinthians 5:17 that anyone who belongs to You has become a new person. The old life is gone; a new life has begun! I declare that my old Way of living is behind me. My old habits, routines, and state of being is dead. I now belong to Jesus. He is first in my life. I exist to serve and glorify Him.

MY SPIRITUAL CLOSET

My closet is full
of God's Designer Label
I wear each daily
making me completely able
to live the life He expects of me
as I prepare for eternity.

Compassion I daily don
my ears to hear, my eyes to see,

LOOSE TO LIVE

A heart that understands,
the plight of my fellow man
gently reaching out to an outstretched hand.

Kindness I consistently wear
to the most vulnerable I must share
even if it's only a smile
making someone's day worthwhile.

Humility is a must
about so many things I can make a fuss
but that's not Christ way at all
on Him daily I must call.

Gentleness is a great wear
aggressiveness I must steer clear
a great disposition I must put on
keeping Jesus always in the forefront.

Patience I had trouble putting on
intolerance was my daily stance
my temper I had to submit
to make me spiritually fit.

Forgiveness was a stretch
but I needed it to be completely dressed
so I poured everything out of my soul
and to my enemies quickly atoned.

Love, though, was easy to wear
I put it on without any fear
I knew it would not be easy to do
but I must love others
before I can love You.

Now my closet is overflowing
filled to the brim with numerous blessings
the more I give the more I get
so there's absolutely nothing to regret
I enjoy dressing each day
in my God's Designer Labels all the way
they daily fill my heart with glee
as I walk my path with pride, faithful to Thee.

HALLELUJAH,

I have found a new life in You. I am no longer who I use to be. I am no longer a slave to sin, a slave to fear, a slave to failure. Thank You that my life is now filled with love, joy, peace, patience, kindness, goodness, faithfulness, gentleness, and self-control. I pray that each one is present and active in my life. I commit my struggle with _____ and pray that it will be brought alive in my life. In Jesus Name, Amen.

DECLARE IT!!!

You declare in Galatians 5:22-23 that the fruit of the Spirit love, joy, peace, patience, kindness, goodness, faithfulness, gentleness, and self-control can be mine. I declare them over my life. I declare that each one is present and active and will be seen in me. In Jesus name, Amen.

Chapter 20

The Change

One of the most difficult things for human beings to do is to embrace *change. Change scares us.* Although change is not always fun, it is necessary as we seek to be transformed into the likeness of Christ in thought, speech, attitude, behaviour and character. As we accept and embrace changes it's important that we release the old thereby providing the perfect opportunity for God to redirect our focus and to get us where He wants us. God has great plans for me …….plans for good and not for disaster, to give me a future and a hope….Jeremiah 29:11.

Are we ready to step into the plans He has in store for us?

NO LONGER A SLAVE…..

I feel like I'm drowning in the sea
Many, many storms have battered me
Waves of destruction I have managed to outrun
I've learnt that I was created to overcome.

Fear has had its way with me
holding me in captivity
stifling my will to be
anything more than ordinary.

Now that Jesus has my heart
He's giving me a brand-new start
daring me daily to see
the greatness inside of me.

Life had a way of pushing my dreams down
burying them beneath discouragement and despondency
mistakes and trials
rejection
inferiority
negativity
feelings of inadequacy
Hiding
the potential
locking it away behind walls of fear.

Today I reject fear
and the torment it
wields over me
the thoughts running through my head
that never, ever seems to end.
but wanting me dead
without ever achieving
anything.

But, fear,
I tell you today
you must leave and go away
far away to stay.
your power is revoked
you are powerless to hold me captive anymore.
today, I say
I need you, no more
goodbye
snare
goodbye, fear.

HALLELUJAH,

Your perfect and complete love has made me whole and has cast out all my fears. Continue Lord to make me fearless, courageous and bold in pursuit of my purpose, my divine destiny. When I get fearful help me not to be paralyzed by my fears, but when I am afraid, help me to trust in You. Help me to trust you more and worry less. In Jesus' Name, Amen.

DECLARE IT!!!

I declare according to 1 Timothy 1:7 that God has not given me a spirit of fear and timidity, but of power, love, and self-discipline. I declare I am no longer a slave to fear according to Psalm 34:4 which says that when I pray to the LORD, He will answer me and free me from all my fears.

DESPAIR TO DELIVERANCE

The Son is a daily reminder that
we can rise again
that from the ashes of sin
we can lift our heads.
It involves a complete shift
in our mindset
a transformation of will
a decision to stop believing lies
about ourselves
about our God
about the real enemy
of our souls.

It is only then
we can find our strength
our voice

our will
our fight
It is only then
we can face
our fears
our doubts
our guilt and shame.

It is only then we learn
to keep conquering
to keep standing
to keep trusting
to keep believing
in Him who sets us free.

only then
will we begin to know
who we are
whose we are
where we are going
Battle Ready

HALLELUJAH,

I thank You that You have broken the spirit of despair over my life. Worry and confusion no longer has dominion and authority over me. I have been set free by the precious blood of my Lord and Saviour, Jesus Christ. Be near me Lord Jesus in my time *of weakness and pain; sustain me by your grace, that my strength and courage may not fail. In Jesus' name, amen.*

DECLARE IT!!!

I declare that I will praise You, You are my God. I will be discouraged no longer; my heart will be sad no more. I will put my hope in You, God. I will praise You my Savior and my God according to Psalm 43:5.

RESTING IN HIM

Trapped
hedged
overwhelmed
no solution in sight?
Darkness looms
no sign of light?

Confronted with a challenge
no resolution?
heavy with doubt
filled with apprehension?

Can't figure out what to do next,
resigned to worry and fret?
on an emotional roller coaster
wondering if things will ever be better?

There is rest for the weary
peace for the troubled mind
there's a home for the wandering one
a place in Him we'll find.
There's power for the powerless
those defenseless and confused
there's help for the helpless
no one He'll refuse.
There's strength for the weak,
joys for the meek
rest for everyone who comes
the Shepherd to seek.

HALLELUJAH!!

Lord, thank you that I can come to you when I'm worn out, tired, weak and overburdened. I choose to believe that You are at work on my behalf. I rest in Your love and Your ability to take care of me. May I always be aware of Your Presence in all that I do and to see Your hand working in every area of my life and when I cannot see Your hand, may I trust Your heart. In Jesus' name, Amen!

DECLARE IT!

I declare that God is my rock and my savior, He is my fortress, my rock, my protector, my shield, my power. My hope comes from him according to Psalm 18:2.

QUIET REST

I used to search for happiness
outside of myself
in the bottle
party
sex
clothes
shoes
bling
things
but I never found it I was a living mess.

But now that I've found Him
realization dawned
happiness cannot
be found
in
things
circumstances
situations
promotions
idolation
adulation
adoration
perfection
no, not at all
these set you up for a fall.

only Him

Him alone

can give to the soul

tranquility

humility

prosperity

serenity

purity

rest

calm

peace

hope

only in Him

can we find

true rest.

HALLELUJAH,

I'm finding rest in You Jesus. You are teaching me how to be calm and relaxed in all circumstances. Thank You for taking all my anxieties, worries and cares. Thank You that when I am tired, when my mind is frazzled, my hands are full, and my emotions are reeling with all the things I have to do, You are teaching me how to cast them all on You. Thank You for reminding me that You are an ever-present help in my times of need. Amen.

DECLARE IT!!!

I declare that my soul waits quietly before God, my victory comes from Him. He alone is my rock and my salvation; He is my fortress, I will never be shaken no matter what may come my way. According to Psalm 62:1-2

PEACE IN CHRIST

We live in a world so chaotic
unstable and unsure
wanting to make us prisoners inside
our own homes.
Time has gotten hard
the days
have become dark
creating fear inside our hearts.
Forbidding us to been out and about
never ever certain how the next minute will work out

Worry and fear have consumed our minds
the peace of God, we struggle to find
and though we know He will never leave us all alone
it's the flesh within us that daily bemoan.
We know that we shouldn't worry about life
should not show fear because of the strife
for in our hearts we know God is protecting
He is the Author of our life, the Father of our destiny

We know
He gives us hope
when hope is gone
He gives us strength
when we can't go on
He gives us shelter from the storms of life
there is always peace in our Saviour, Jesus Christ

His peace
brings stability to our minds
creating calmness deep inside,
for that is what we desperately need
in this world so cold and mired in greed

So when we have those stressful days,
when the hours are dark and there are no sun rays
allow God's peace to calm and soothe
and know that in Him we can never lose
if we but rest in His Amazing grace
and allow
His peace to fill our space.

HALLELUJAH,

Thank You for giving me peace of mind and calmness for my troubled heart. Thank You that when I am tempted to worry constantly that Your peace is available. Dress me every day with strength and clarity of mind to find my purpose and walk the path You've laid out for me. I trust Your love, plans and purpose for my life. In Jesus name, Amen.

DECLARE IT!!!

I will not give place to worry, confusion, instability. God's peace is within me, not the world's peace but the peace which comes from above. I will not let my heart be troubled, neither will I let it be afraid. My words, thoughts, and imaginations are under the power of Christ.

PHENOMENAL WOMAN

A phenomenal woman kneels each day to pray,
knowing God's grace will keep her soul in the right way
professing spiritual exercise is a must
she spends time with God with no fuss.
for she knows spiritual laziness is not the way
to grow in grace day by day.

A Phenomenal woman
lives by faith and not fear
always knowing her God is near
she trust His plans for her life
keeping her purpose always in clear sight
she knows God's plan is full and complete
so she trusts Him, never fearing defeat.

A Phenomenal woman
walks in complete authority
knowing heaven is her destiny
so she centers her mind on things above
basking in her Redeemer's love
knowing that for the journey she'll have enough,
though sometimes life will get really rough,
she knows the storms will sometimes stay for long
But in Jesus she will always remain strong.

A Phenomenal woman
knows it's not about the bling and stuff,
that will aid her when things get toughIt's her relationship
with Jesus Christ
that will anchor and steers her life.
It's her resilience
her ability to rise
from the ashes of the earth
the rubble of the dirt
knowing He'll always be there
for He'll never leave
her side.

HALLELUJAH,

You are an amazing God who is seeking to accomplish extraordinary things in me and through me. Thank You for releasing me from self-imposed limitations, fears and failures. Thank

You for breaking every limitation that the enemy has placed upon my life. Lord, Your Word says, I am more precious than rubies. (Prov. 31:10) and in the name of Jesus, I loose myself from every limitation, barrier, obstruction that has kept me from meeting my full potential and becoming that gem I was created to be. Decades of oppression and failure will come to an end. In Jesus Name, Amen.

DECLARE IT!!!

I declare today that I am God's masterpiece according to Eph. 2:10. I am Beautiful, Valuable, Amazing, Phenomenal. You have created me anew in You so I can do the good things You planned for me long ago. Your workmanship is marvelous Psalm 139:13.

DIVINE LEGACY

Our legacy
what will it be?
What will happen
after we die
and many cry?
Will we just be lowered in the ground
leaving no influence around.
Nothing for future generations to see
nothing to influence eternity?

LOOSE TO LIVE

Will we be missed
or will we just exit earth
as quietly as was our birth?
What will we leave behind
that will influence the minds
of
young and
old
men and
women
boys and
girls?

What will we be known for?
missed for?
what vacuum will we
leave in this world?
what footprints will we leave
on the seashore of time?
what trail would we have set ablaze?
what awareness did we raise?

Whose lives will our story
touch?
did we live a life of purpose
seeking to make a difference in this world
did we seek to shape color and creed
Did we teach?
Did we learn?
Did we lead?

HALLELUJAH,

I was not created to just exist, to just occupy a space on this earth. I was created for a purpose. To influence change, to blaze a trail, to touch lives and to facilitate change in the lives of those I come in contact with. May I never become comfortable with just merely existing. May I never just blend in, help me to always allow You to shine through me. In Jesus name, Amen.

DECLARE IT!!!

I declare that I will leave an inheritance, a legacy for those coming after me. According to Proverbs 13:22 which says Good people leave an inheritance to their grandchildren.

MOVING BEYOND THE TRAJECTORY

We still live in a century
where women are relegated
to who many think we should be
we don't say it
but many think we are misfits
in what some perceive to be
a male dominated world.

Deep in the hearts of many
women should be nursing babies
keeping the house clean
cooking her mate's meal

keeping it hot
on the stove top
until he gets home
from a hard day at work.

But we have grown past that era
and as women we are in every area
dominating our fields
gaining great yields
proving we are as good
or better than
any man.

It's clear
we can have it all
career
home
babies
businesses
without losing a sense of who we are
who we were created to be
women
independent
strong
successful
accomplished.

HALLELUJAH,

I can do all things through Christ who strengthens me. Thank You that I can accomplish anything even those things that may seem impossible. Help me to be relentless about those pursuits I'm passionate about. Take away all signs of complacency, procrastinating, mediocrity, laziness and the attitude which gives up easily. Help me if and when I fall to always get up and try again. In Jesus name, Amen.

DECLARE IT!!!

Your Word declares that I can do everything through Christ, who gives me strength. Philippians 4:13. I am empowered to endure all things, to rejoice as God enables me, by His power and grace, to endure and achieve in both good times and bad. I wake up with purpose, direction, and meaning every day of my life.

Chapter 21

Tributes

While society emphasizes wealth, success, and the pursuit of pleasure, the truth is that we are created by God in His image, and our fulfillment is found in pursuing His will for our lives. I encourage all women – whether you are mothers and wives, single mothers, barren women, women who work outside the home, older women, younger women, abused women, victimized women...... God's daughters everywhere to embrace God's purpose for your lives.....Arise, break free, break forth into purpose!!!

BECOMING THE SIGNATURE WOMAN
(For my daughter)

From the day you were born
your purpose on this earth was clear
you were destined to bring laughter, pride and joy
To many far and near.
You have not disappointed
from your divine appointment
as you have grown to be
the embodiment of pride, joy and beauty.

As you begin your growth to womanhood, this fact you must know,
you'll always be my source of pride, no matter where you go.
stand tall and proud, within you feel no fear,
for all you dreams are right before you- very, very near.
Continue to be compassionate, always lend a hand
never be judgmental, seek first to understand.

You are living your dream
as young as you are
rising to the top
knowing you were born a star.
You will shine
as long as you give your all
you shall rise each time you fall.

Don't ever give up
though the road may seem hard
always rise with purpose
God is your Guide and Guard.
Know that each failure will make you strong
and I'll always be there to help you along.
Continue to be diligent
never settle for mediocrity
Be persistent and consistent
work with great alacrity
allow tenacity to always be your guide
the principle on which you abide.

As you choose your career
aim to be the very best
work hard, pray hard
divine favour will do the rest.
shoot for the top
never, ever stop
nor settle for just a 'tiny drop.'

And when you chose your husband
never settle for second best
you must be his number one
with great love and respect.
Accept nothing less than what you deserve
be confident, poised, savvy happy in your skin
always pulling from the beauty that lies deep within.

You know God's love
you have experienced His grace
never allow yourself to be driven from His face
desire Him, yearn for Him, chase after Him,
find your completion and fulfillment in Him
Make Him a priority in your life
in all you acquire stay with God my child
live by His Word; allow it to be your guide.
With God's love in your heart and the world by its tail,
you'll always be a winner, and victory will prevail.

HALLELUJAH,

You wove this child in my womb. You made her with fear and wonder; marvelous are Your works, You know her completely. Her frame was not hidden from You when she was made. Your eyes saw her unformed body and You designed a plan for her long ago. Your plans for her life are settled in heaven and no plans of Yours, Lord can be thwarted. Thank You that You have the power to bring to pass that which You promised. So I commit her in Your hands knowing that as long as she keeps her eyes on You her future is secured. In Jesus name, Amen

DECLARE IT!!!

I decree and declare that the plans You have for _____ life cannot be altered and thwarted. I declare that Your plans for her are settled in heaven and every single one will be realized. There will be no derailment, no missed opportunity, and no regretful actions. In Jesus name, amen.

POWERFUL WOMEN

We rose from the ashes of humanity
knowing the top was our destiny
from slave plantations
we've survived the intentions
of powerful men and women
to annihilate us
wipe us out
make us non-existent
But
we could not
and cannot
be stopped
we are indomitable
formidable
unbreakable.

So despite carefully crafted oppression
in stubborn rebellion
we continue
to rise and rise and rise.

We've defied slavery
racism
rape
neglect
abuse of every kind
inflicted on our bodies, thoughts and minds.

We've give birth to
great ideas and inventions
leadership and creations.
We continue to rise
above limitations
borders
boundaries
soaring to new heights
In Christ
realizing that each achievement
is just an outward manifestation
of divine destiny.

HALLELUJAH,

I am powerful in Jesus Christ. I am growing in the grace and in knowledge of Jesus so that my actions and attitudes reflect His grace. Empower me to fulfill my mission and purpose in life, dear Father. Help me to be a capable, intelligent, and virtuous woman – faithful, diligent, generous and spiritually strong. I am determined to continually allow Your Word to dwell in me richly. As I grow in Your Word, help me to always be obedient to You and to Your will in every area of my life. I commit myself to pursuing Your purpose for my life. In Jesus' Name, Amen.

DECLARE IT!!!

I declare that I am empowered, capable, intelligent, virtuous, faithful, diligent, generous and spiritually strong.

SIGNATURE WOMAN...CONNECTIONS

There's something powerful
that takes place when women get together,
It's more than making connections
It's an igniting of each other.
It's that electric atmosphere
that becomes palpable in the air
It is especially obvious
with women who have experienced GRACE.

There is so much power
in the stories that are told
amazing resilience as the experiences
unfold.
As women share their lives of failures and defeat
falling, bruising yet rising stronger
to their feet.
The many struggles that as women we
go through
struggles meant to overpower
but instead empower
me and you.

it's a deep gladness
galvanized sometimes by deep sadness
an admission that as difficult as life gets
we can journey through it with very
little regret.

Signature women, living life
together
gathering once a year, connecting with
each other.
It's a freeing moment, exhilarating and refreshing
a time of utter abandon, giving and receiving,
openly worshipping our Master and King
emptying ourselves, giving Him everything
Allowing him to replenish us
By making us strong within.
Then we say our goodbyes
Sometimes with sad and teary eyes
but knowing
we are ready to face the world, we are not alone
Jesus is alive and still on the throne
He has our back...

HALLELUJAH,

We do not have to walk this journey alone. Thank You for preparing various avenues for me to be supported in my walk with You. Thank You for the bold women who provide forums and conferences where we can receive inspiration, motivation and support.

DECLARE IT!!!

I declare that I am not alone. I do not need to walk alone. There is someone to stand in the gap for me. There is someone to intercede on my behalf.

MY STORY…YOUR STORY

You removed the veil that clouded my eyes
closed my ears to all the enemy's empty promises and lies
now I can see what's real
how my joy he would rob and steal
but no more
I've had enough
now I have a God-shaped hole in my heart
—nothing fills it
nothing…but Him.

God's plans and purposes flow beautifully
through the scriptures
each one carefully crafted,
each one completely reliable.
I'm learning,
there is nothing random or spontaneous about Him
nothing careless about His works
He is purposeful in all things
working deep within
enabling me to be
the very best 'me.'

He has reserved for me a future filled with hope a plan perfectly formulated with my name on it.
A plan written long my birth
A plan built upon the gifts and talent
He has laden me with.

A plan to make me
joyful, not miserable
fruitful, not destitute
rich, not poor
victorious, not defeated
prospering in all things.
a good plan
a perfect plan
a complete plan
with a victory already won.

I'm tapping into His purpose for me.
understanding that my story is part of a bigger story
A greater story
a grander story
His story
my story
our story
laced with eternity
lived out on earth
understanding this great insight
has become my guiding light.

HALLELUJAH,

I know that You can do all things; no one can stop your plans. Job 42:2b. Before I was formed in my mother's womb you knew me and had a perfect plan for my life. I trust Your plans and purposes for me. In Jesus name, Amen.

DECLARE IT!!!

I declare that in You I am unstoppable, unshakable, secured, firmed. I am the daughter of the King of all kings. Because of Jesus, I lack nothing. You have given me everything I need to do what You've called me to do. I wake up with purpose, direction, and meaning every day of my life.

PHENOMENAL YOU
MY SISTER WHO MOTHERED ME

I will never take for granted
The role you played in my life
when you choose to mother me
though you were barely a child.

It was not your job
yet you nurtured me with great care
And every time I've needed you
you were always there.

I never would have made it
had you not taken me in
had you not sacrificed your life
to give to me everything.

You are more than my sister
you are my best friend
you are the one who was always there
when my heart needs to mend.

You're my role model
the perfect mother
strong, purposeful
elegant, go-getter.

I saw in you all I aspired to be
grace, poise
compassion, independence
determination, beauty.

You are and will always be my angel in disguise.
intuitive, fashionable, intelligent and wise.
always giving and helping me through
good times and bad.
you are the greatest mom/sister a girl could ever have had.

HALLELUJAH,

Lord, thank you so much for what you've given me. I feel blessed for the life that I have and the people you've placed in it. I thank you for my sister (aunt, cousin) _____. Bless her and guide her footsteps toward a bright future full of love and <u>hope</u>. As she has stretched forth her hands to give unselfishly, I pray that you will bless her a hundred-fold. In Jesus name, amen.

DECLARE IT!!!

2 Cor. 9:8 declares that God will generously provide all the needs of _____. That she will always have everything she needs and have plenty left over to share with others.

About the Author

Chevonette James-Henry resides in Kingston, Jamaica. She holds a diploma in Early Childhood Education and a B.Ed in Special Education (Western Carolina University). She is currently a special education teacher at the STEP Centre. She is a Married to Andrew Henry and is mother to Jon-Mark, Jor-Dan and Joi-Ann. Her passion is to inspire and motivate each person to recognize the greatness that lies within them. She's the author of the books *Defying the Odds, CP and Me*, and the *Loose to Live Journal*.

www.ingramcontent.com/pod-product-compliance
Lightning Source LLC
Chambersburg PA
CBHW062149080426
42734CB00010B/1622